FRAME UP!

FRAME UP!

A Story of Essex, its Shipyards and its People

Dana Story

CHARLESTON   LONDON

History
PRESS

Dedicated to Margaret

Published by The History Press
18 Percy Street
Charleston, South Carolina 29403

866.223.5778
www.historypress.net

Published in this edition 2004

Manufactured in the United Kingdom

ISBN: 1-59629-019-6

Library of Congress CIP data applied for

Cover images:
Front: FRAME UP! Raising a frame on the keel of the *Kingfisher* in 1946.
Back: Twenty-seven-year-old Dana A. Story stands in the doorway of the Story Shipyard shop,
May 20, 1946.

contents

Acknowledgements

The author is much indebted to Mr. Edwin C. Perkins, Sr., Mr. John P. Story, Mr. Thomas Boutchie, Sr., Mr. Edwin H. Oxner, Mr. Lewis H. Story and Mr. Palmer S. Perkins, all of whom are now gone, for a great number of the stories, recollections and information contained herein. Some, especially Mr. Edwin Perkins, gave me literally hours and hours of their time in the preparation of my notes. For the help and recollections of others of my friends and fellow townsmen, Mr. Marshall H. Cogswell, Mr. George Story, Mr. John Doyle, Mr. Peter Hubbard, Mr. Theodore S. Burnham, Mr. A. Stanley Wonson, Mr. Elbridge Perkins, Mr. Roswell Low, Mr. Scott Lambert and Mr. Frederick L. W. Richardson Jr., I am also grateful.

I wish particularly to express my thanks to Mr. George S. McIntire for his invaluable help in supplying me with much of my historical background as well as many of the stories, and also to my friend, Mr. Raymond S. Stoddard, for the uncounted hours he devoted to the typing of the manuscript. The author has also made reference to the following publications:

History of the Town of Essex by Reverend Robert Crowell. Published by Town of Essex in 1868.
John Wise—Early American Democrat by George Allan Cook. Published by *Columbia* University in 1952.

Builders of Gloucester's Prosperity by Gordon W. Thomas. Published by Cape Ann Savings Bank in 1952.

Dana A. Story
Essex, Massachusetts
1963

Foreword

Perhaps the reason why the people of America, and particularly of New England, have recently been so preoccupied with the history of their country and with life as it used to be is that things have changed so rapidly in our country. Ways of living, modes of transportation, fashions of dress and whole industries have come and gone in a few short generations. The face of the landscape is, in so many cases, completely changed from what it was even fifty years ago. No wonder, then, that many of us look back with longing to the times now gone much as a traveler does as he leaves forever the familiar scenes of his homeland or his childhood.

Many books and articles have been written and will continue to be written about the so-called good old days. People will always love to tell of the things they used to do and how things used to be. Much of this makes very interesting and enjoyable reading. In an age of atoms, rockets and outer space such reflection induces feelings of nostalgia even among those who never actually experienced the events described. There is a warmth and security to these memories, which resembles in many ways the anchor holding onto the storm-tossed ship.

It has occurred to me that I ought to write something about Essex because Essex has a history, which is not only interesting but is unquestionably unique among old American towns. Furthermore, it begins to look as though nobody else will do it if I don't, and others beside myself have felt that there are many informative and amusing stories here to tell.

Therefore I will present in the pages to come a gathering of recollections concerning our town, its life, its people and its ships. Many of them are my own; more of them have been passed on to me by those to whom they were first-hand experience. Some of the material contained herein is also, of course, a matter of historical record. All this is not intended to be in any sense a scholarly treatise.

By way of giving a brief bit of background and to set the stage, so to speak, for these chapters, I might say that this town of Essex is situated just to the north of Cape Ann and its famous port of Gloucester, and lies up a small tidewater river which is designated quite appropriately as Essex River. The town of Essex was incorporated and so named in the year 1819, having previously been a part of the town of Ipswich, and known as Chebacco Parish in Ipswich, or simply, Chebacco. The first settlers arrived here, however, in the year 1634.

The dominant activity of Essex people has, until very late years, been the building of boats and ships of which a prodigious number have sailed away down our river. Were it not for this fact there would be little to distinguish the town from the hundreds of other rustic New England communities about which volumes have already been written. It was the ships and the men who built them which gave Essex a flavor of its own and which now make for some interesting story telling.

It will be noted as we go along that I use the terms: boat, ship and vessel. It would seem before going further that it might be well to clarify these terms somewhat. Through custom we have referred to the boats built here as "ships" principally because they were always very heavily constructed and because for the last hundred years or so they averaged 90 to 100 feet in length. Of course, in the early times, they weren't as big as that, but in later years many were much bigger, even approaching 200 feet in length and more than 30 feet of beam. Generally, "boat" refers to a smaller craft of light construction. In Essex, "vessel" is the commonly used term applied to any of the wooden ships we have built.

The usual connotation of "frame-up" is a kind of questionable scheme that somebody devises to place the blame for off-color shenanigans onto someone else. To those of us who were born and brought up in Essex, in the days when we built vessels here, "Frame-up" was the stirring cry that went out from a framing stage when one of a vessel's frames had been put together and was ready to be raised. In building a wooden vessel, the frames, or ribs as they are often called, are assembled and fastened together on a staging built along the new keel. When the frame, which of course is lying there on the stage is finished, the leader of the framing gang hollers, "Frame-up!" and all the rest of the men in the shipyard

The schooner *Angeline C. Noonan*, built in 1913 is shown in the framing stage.

FRAME UP! Raising a frame on the keel of the *Kingfisher* in 1946.

drop whatever they're doing for a few minutes and go over to help the framing gang stand the thing up on top of the keel. This is accomplished by the simple expedient of stooping over, all together, grabbing it and heaving and pushing until it's up.

When it is considered that so far as any documentary evidence shows, there are records of over three thousand three hundred wooden ships built in Essex, plus perhaps half again as many of which no formal record is preserved, and when it is also considered that each one of these had perhaps an average of 40 or more frames, it can be understood that the cry "Frame-up" became a part and a symbol of a way of life which now has disappeared from our town and has, in fact, disappeared from the whole American scene.

one

Historical Background

Beside the causeway which runs between Essex and South Essex is an historical tablet placed there in 1930 by the Commonwealth of Massachusetts, which reads:

SHIPYARD OF 1668

In 1668 the town granted the adjacent acre of land "to the inhabitants of Ipswich for a yard to build vessels and to employ workmen for that end". Shipbuilding has continued uninterruptedly in Essex since that date.

That there was enough shipbuilding going on in this Chebacco Parish of Ipswich by the year 1668 to warrant such a move by the town would indicate that shipbuilding here actually had its beginning some years before. We know as a matter of record that the first saw mill in town was built along the river in 1656 and by 1667 there were three of them, so it is only natural to assume that some of the products of these mills were going into boats. In fact, Crowell in his History of Essex says: "Probably the building of vessels here was the reason why so many saw mills were erected."

Tradition has it that the town's first boat was built in the garret of his house by a man named Burnham and that it was necessary to tear out the end of the house before she could be launched. The story goes on to say, moreover, that the following summer two Burnhams, man and boy, sailed this boat 120 miles down the Maine coast for a fare of fish. It is not known by actual count how many boats have been built in Essex. In the beginning records were not kept. Later on, when documentation of vessels was started, the records were incomplete and now, of course, many of these are lost. As I mentioned in the foreword, we do have records beginning about 1785 of over three thousand Essex vessels, and an estimated total of over four thousand does not seem unreasonable. Statistics are not particularly important in themselves. What is of interest here is the fact of a little country town becoming so devoted to the building of ships that at length it was said that one out of every twenty-eight ships of *all descriptions* flying the American flag was built in Essex. It would appear, therefore, that the town of Essex has a unique history and tradition such as few other places in the world possess. Indeed we have a past of which many of the present residents of the town are unaware.

In late years feature writers of the country's papers and magazines often seized upon Essex and its shipyards as picturesque throwbacks to the industry of colonial days. We were portrayed so many times as a bunch of unlettered boobs who whiled away the sunny hours hewing out staunch wooden ships (for iron men to sail in) while the rest of the world went by. About the only purpose served by such stuff was to attract the curious and present them with an opportunity to ask lots of silly questions.

Let me point out that the process by which a wooden ship is built differs little even today from the methods of Colonial or yet Biblical times. It is largely a series of hand operations. Therefore, it is easy to see, as times progressed, how we would appear as something of an anachronism. Here we had men wielding broad-axes and adzes and putting a ship together a piece at a time while else where, for example, automobiles were being stamped out by the million. I acknowledge, too, that in our pastoral setting we undoubtedly were picturesque as industries go. Yet as far as we ourselves were concerned, we were only doing here what we knew and loved, and incidentally, trying to make a living along the way.

In the beginning, Essex built its boats strictly for its own use. Land around here was hostile to agriculture and close proximity to the ocean and its abundance of fish induced the settlers to try their luck at fishing. This meant that they had to build boats. The Essex River (or Chebacco River, as it was then) is a narrow winding and tidal affair extending five miles in from Ipswich Bay, so the boats couldn't be very large if they were to sail in and out of the river. Also, they were meant to be handled by no more than two or three men. There were practically limitless stands of virgin timber growing almost to the water's edge so the shipbuilding industry naturally flourished once it became established.

The reputation of the Chebacco men and their boats spread quickly and before many years the yards here were building boats for the fishermen of neighboring communities. Chief among these was Gloucester. Here was a town that was to become one of the most famous fishing and maritime communities on earth, yet the great majority of the ships it used were built in Essex.

The history of the shipbuilding industry as such in Chebacco, later to become Essex, was pretty much a gradual progression of size and numbers—both numbers of ships and numbers of building yards. Numerous types of fishing boats were evolved and achieved wide recognition. There were the Chebacco boats (middle and later 1700's), dogbodies (approximately 1800), pinkies (about 1820), and finally the more familiar schooners. Several books have been written which treat of the technical aspects of these developments for those who are interested. Mr. Howard I. Chappelle, now of the Smithsonian Institution, has traced the evolution of the local ships with scholarly care and detail.

In the decades immediately preceding and following the Civil War, the Essex shipyards came into their own. Every available plot of solid land adjoining the otherwise marshy banks of the channel was utilized as a building yard. Sailing vessels, fishing schooners, steamers, yachts and three-masted coasters came down the ways by the hundreds. What a sight it must have been to see all the ships taking form. One could stand along the causeway in the center of town, turn in any direction and see vessels on the stocks. In 1852 there were fifteen different shipyards in town and in the year from November 1851 to November 1852, sixty vessels were built.

In the 1870's and early 80's, some of the vessels being built had become so large that it was barely possible to get them out of the river. The *Hattie N. Bangs* measured 571 gross tons; the *Ida C. Bullard* 549, the *Mattie W. Atwood* 653, and biggest of all, *Vidette*, measured 810 gross tons. This last was a steam collier 191 feet long, 34 feet wide, 17 feet depth of hold and was built for Mr. Lamont G. Burnham who left Essex as a young man to found and head Boston's Metropolitan Coal Company. With boats such as these it often took the combined efforts of two tugs over a period of two or three tides to take them down the river. They would go along until they stuck in the mud, usually to stay there until the high tide came again to float them.

The great majority of the Essex boats were, of course, the fishing schooners. Averaging 90 to 100 feet or more in length, they came from all the many shipyards. In South Essex were the yards of several of the Burnhams. There were Willard R., Willard A., Daniel, Aaron and Ebenezer; also, Benjamin Courtney and

Charles Parkhurst. Later on came Oxner and Story, Leonard MacKenzie, and Owen Lantz. Along the causeway were the yards of Andrew Story and the great firm of John James and Co. In Essex center were the yards of Oliver Burnham, Luke Burnham, Epes Story, Abel Story, Job Story, Joseph Story, Moses Adams, and Arthur D. Story, which last is the only one still to operate. In the north part of town on a small tidal inlet was yet another yard operated at times by Thomas Hardy and by Parker Burnham.

Building yards were not confined to sites along the water's edge. There were several spots, particularly in what is now Essex Falls, where smaller vessels were built, sometimes a mile or more from the river. When completed they were placed on sets of crude wheels to be pulled to the launching site by several teams of oxen. It was the custom for the townspeople to make something of a holiday of these events, pitching in to help and then to join in the fun as the new boat hit the water.

It should be borne in mind that not all of these builders were operating at the same time. Some took up the business where others left off. The firm of Oxner and Story began in 1900 in the yard formerly used by Mr. Willard A. Burnham. (He, incidentally, was the son of Willard R. Burnham.) A rock-bound Republican, Mr. Burnham, commonly known as Willard Alvin, had decided prior to the election of 1892 that if the Democrats won, the country was headed for economic ruin and shipbuilding would undoubtedly cease. So when Grover Cleveland went back to the White House for his second term, Willard Alvin gave up. Mr. Arthur D. Story, of whom we shall speak later, occupied at the height of his career what had previously been four different yards, one of which being that of his father Job Story and grandfather, Abel Story.

Let us digress for a moment and take passing note of these names. It was not unusual years ago for almost the total population of small country towns to have maybe four or five basic family names with only a few miscellaneous outsiders thrown in. In Essex, as might be seen, the names were, first of all Burnham, then Story and Andrews, with somewhat smaller numbers of Choates, Cogswells, Perkinses and Lows. Even today there are more Burnhams in the Essex phone book than any other name.

There used to be an old minstrel show joke which said that if a total stranger were to walk up Main Street he could say to the first man he met, "Good morning, Mr. Burnham". If the man didn't answer, he could say, "Good morning, Mr. Andrews". If the man still didn't answer, he could say, "Good morning, Mr. Story" and by gorrie, he'd have to answer!

18

As might be imagined, the large number of people with the same last name made things a little confusing to the outsider or the newcomer to town. Natives weren't much bothered because they had been brought up in it and had a little system that designated the various individuals. It was simple. All you did was call a man (or woman) by his first two names, or his first name and middle initial, or his first name and father's first name, or his first name and father's nick-name or even by his name and where he came from. This, of course, was if he happened to have a regular Essex name but moved into town from somewhere else. You automatically knew last names by virtue of having lived here all your life.

Thus we had John Prince, Frank White and Sam Lewis (Story—no relation); Henry Clarence, Charlie Gus and Frank Ellis (Burnham—no relation); Charley Berry and Henry Clay (Cogswell—no relation); Lucy Zack (Burnham—so-called be cause her father's name was Zaccheus); Charley Sam (his name was Story and his father's name was Samuel); Frank N. (Burnham), Lewis I. (Andrews), Cy Israel (Andrews) or George Hamilton (Story—so-called because he came to Essex from Hamilton). Then, just to make things interesting, we had Fred M. (Burnham), Fred K. (Burnham), Fred Ephraim (Andrews), Eddie James (Story) and Johnny Frank (James). Imagine what it was like when girls married into families of the same name. It often happened. Lots of people who have moved to Essex in recent years have lived here quite a while without knowing that some of those to whom they spoke every day had real names quite different from those by which they were commonly called.

No doubt all this intermarrying among the same families for so many years had its effect in the number of queers or skew pods that appeared. We Storys had our share. One in particular was Pierpont Story, commonly known as Pip. Pip used to go fishing from an upstairs window into a bucket below on the ground. Then there was Charley Foster who would lie on his stomach cutting the grass with scissors and stuffing it in a burlap bag. There was also the one they called Crazy Nathan. His name was Andrews. It is said that he was once charged by an angry bull but grabbed the beast by the forelegs and actually held him until help arrived. I remember him as an old man who shuffled along the sidewalk and whose standard greetings were, "Colder'n common, ain't it!" or "How's your old 'gruh?'" I never did find out what he meant by "gruh."

Let us examine some of the actual workings of an old time shipyard and see something of the ways in which they operated. The picture of a shipyard, which appears to most people's minds in our present day, is one of a large industrial complex with shops and docks and giant cranes swinging overhead. How different things were in our town 60 or 70 years ago.

The shipyard was actually no more than that; just a plot of ground big enough to set two or three vessels on with a little more room for a place to put the timber and build a small shop. Even a shop was not perhaps absolutely necessary, but it was convenient to have a place in which the men could put their tool chests and also to store spikes, paint and the small amount of miscellaneous gear that belonged to the yard. In short, everything about the operation was literally done by hand. Oh, there was sometimes a horse or an ox to do heavy pulling but that was all. To the best of my knowledge, the first machinery of any kind introduced into an Essex shipyard came in 1884 when Moses Adams bought a band saw and set up a steam engine and boiler to run it. Even then the other yards were slow to adopt it, although they finally were forced to follow suit. Some, however, went out of business rather than be bothered with any such new-fangled affairs as this.

Any man who went to work in the yards was a real mechanic and was expected to own any tools which he might he required to use. Many of the men, however, were specialists in some particular phase of the operation and necessary tool requirements were usually fairly simple. So it can be seen that to establish a shipyard in the early days all a man needed was an order to build a boat, a place to set things up and a few men to do the work.

Financing was not much of a problem since the men were not paid in full until the builder was paid for his work. A captain ordering a boat customarily made a down payment of enough money to buy the lumber. The men would receive a little money each week—how much depended on the financial standing of the builder—and would wait until the vessel was finished before receiving the balance of their wages. These, by the way, in the 70's and 80's averaged for the journeyman about $2.00 a day in busy times or $1.75 to $1.85 if times were dull. A day was divided into quarters for purposes of time keeping and the workweek consisted in the early years of six 10-hour days, later reduced, following a brief strike, to nine hours.

One cannot help but wonder in this day and age how it was possible for a working man to go along, perhaps for months, without getting regular wages. This, however, had a simple solution. The family kept a little notebook that was taken along to the general store every time anything was needed there. The storekeeper listed in the book whatever was bought and every six months or even once a year the book was brought in to be totaled up and settlement made. Sometimes the operator of a shipyard himself kept the store, doing business with his men and making appropriate adjustments in their wages. Many are the ship carpenters who built and maintained good homes and raised sizable families on cash incomes of but a few hundred dollars a year.

The nine hour day carried on until about 1910 when the men in the Gloucester yards and later the Essex yards struck again; this time for eight hours, although still continuing to work six days a week. On this occasion a committee of the men was delegated to go in and see Mr. John Bishop who operated the only large yard in Gloucester.

"What do you want, boys?" said Mr. Bishop.

"Meest Bishop," said the spokesman who was a French Canadian, "we decided we gonna work eight hours!"

"That so?" said Mr. Bishop. "Well, I'm damn glad to hear it."

And that's all there was to that.

In Essex it was almost the same. A.D. Story came back to the yard one noon after dinner to find the gang sitting around.

"Well," he said, "What's the matter?"

"Arthur," said someone, "we're striking for eight hours."

"Well, that's all right," said Arthur. "What are you waiting for?"

Arthur, likewise, was a man of few words.

Although the workday became eight hours, the workweek continued to be six days well into the 1930's when seemingly by common consent it eventually was reduced to five and one-half days. It was not of any great significance, however, since hourly rates of pay had come into general use some years before.

Thus we have traced some of the highlights in the history of Essex shipbuilding through the years. It was unquestionably the main stem of life and industry in the town right up to the year 1932. At that time the death of one of the town's leading builders and the onslaught of the Great Depression joined forces to close temporarily the town's two remaining yards. While both were to operate spasmodically for a few more years and World War II with its succeeding boom stimulated a burst of renewed activity, the end was soon to come and in June of 1949 the last vessel was launched into the Essex River from an Essex shipyard. Quite appropriately, she was a beautiful little schooner, and her departure closed the book on a remarkable era in the life of a remarkable town.

two

The Men

A S WE HAVE SEEN, AN Essex shipyard in the old days was hardly a remarkable place as far as its physical characteristics, location or equipment were concerned. What really made the place was the collection of men who worked there. It was they who, with their hands, created the ships, gave them the form and grace they possessed and made them by their straining, sweat and even by their curses the personalities by which the ships came to be known. Anyone who has ever been intimate with a ship, be it large or small, knows it has a personality and moreover that such personality is unmistakably feminine. (I have never gotten used to the notion of naming a ship for a man. It just doesn't fit.)

In any given group there is always a variety of temperament. Briefly, I think, the disposition or temperament of all people divides itself into two classes: those who have a sense of humor and those who don't. Among the men who worked in the Essex shipyards I would say that the great majority of them belonged (perhaps of necessity) to the group with the sense of humor. That is why the recollection of those days and those people is so pleasant. A sense of humor gave zest and uplift to long days and years of difficult and arduous toil for which the material reward was always pitiably small. Many is the Essex man who has stayed to work in the yards at home, attracted perhaps by the spirit of the thing, when he could easily have gone elsewhere for twice the wages he got here.

The French Canadians of Nova Scotia were the first group to provide a new influx of people to the population of Essex. It gave the Burnhams, Storys,

Choates and Andrewses a jolt to find names like Boutchie, Muise, LeBlanc and Doucette cropping up among them. The Canadian people began to come in the middle 1890's and were not long in taking up work in the shipyards. They came by it naturally since many had worked in the yards "down home" and others had sailed for years as fishermen in the Essex built schooners. They were quickly accepted for they proved to be hard and willing workers, and moreover they contributed much to the spirit and humor of life in town and work in the yards. They were willing and able to make many jokes themselves as well as to be the butt of as many more.

The story is told of a rather bashful soul who, just arrived from "down home", was staying with relatives in Gloucester. They told him to come over to Essex and try for a job in the shipyards, suggesting further that he start with my father. He disappeared and was gone most of the day. When he finally came back they asked if he had seen Mr. Story. "Yes, I seen heem," was the reply. "Well, what did he say?" they asked. "I dunno," he answered, "I deen' speak to heem and he deen' answer me!"

There was another one who had the misfortune to suffer a bad accident after being up here a while and as he lay in the hospital he asked a nurse if she would please write to his sister down home. "What shall I say?" asked the nurse. "Write and say, My dear sis, my dear lovely—I have bad accident and am flat on my back. Bode my legs break. Hope dis letter finds you de same. If you can't come in de one boat come in de two. You loving brudder."

We used to have trolley cars in Essex that ran both to Beverly and to Gloucester. When a certain point along the route known as "end of the limit" was reached the cars stopped while the conductor came around to collect another 5-cent fare. A "down homer" who had paid his first 5 cents for a trip and who unknowingly had reached one of these points was startled one day to see the conductor standing before him demanding another nickel. "What?" he roared. "Five cents where you come from—five cents where you go to! How de hell dat is?"

The prize remark was gotten off by Dennis Martin one day when he stopped in at Joe Garvins' grocery store on his way home from work. Peering into the show case for something to eat he spied a pastry toward the back and pointing at it yelled to Joe, "What kinda cookie you call dem cake dare, Joe, fig bar?"

There was John Prince Story who, though well over 90, would meet his friend Tom Boutchie every afternoon in the Post Office.

At 96 Tom's mind was keen as a whip and he had a ready answer for all comers. John liked to try and insult Tom but he never could get the last word. He said to Tom one day, "You know, Tom, things went along fine in Essex till that gang started coming up from down Novy. Then," he said, "things began to quiet right down." "Twarn't no wonder", replied Tom. "They worked twice as hard as this old crowd around here ever did, and it wasn't no time 'fore all the jobs was finished up!" Then, as a parting shot, Tom said, "Tell me, John, ees eet true dey drove de Storys out of England for stealin' sheep?"

One of the more notable of French ship carpenters of late years was a fellow named Phil Terrio. I suppose his name originally was spelled "Theriault" but he shortened it so that it was easier to pronounce and to spell. He was a born actor and would tell stories by the hour if you would let him. As a young man he rode around town in a sulky. He had a hole through the septum of his nose and with a little urging from us kids would turn his back, make a few mysterious flourishes, and whirl around again with a great spike right though his nose and a grin from ear to ear.

Phil always had trouble with his wife. She pretty much ruled the roost at home so that in the last years of his working, his employers took pity on him and gave him two pay envelopes on Saturday: one to take home to the old lady and one for Phil to use in satisfying a few personal needs for tobacco or beer.

Phil once bought a tombstone for his wife's first husband. He liked to tell what a fine fellow he was to do this for her. "You holy S.O.B.", somebody said to him one day, "you only put it there so the old man wouldn't get up!" "Is that so?" answered Phil. "I wish the bastard would get up and come take his old job back!"

Phil couldn't write and when he got dry he would send over to the package store for a pint of wine, giving the messenger a chip marked with a cross that was to be redeemed at the end of the week. It wasn't long before others in the gang caught on to this and when Phil went over to pay off, here was a whole basket of chips, all marked with an "X". Poor Phil had to pay. I think Phil's favorite story was about the Irishman who bought some acid in a drugstore under the mistaken impression he was getting medicinal whiskey. Asked how he liked it, he said he hadn't tasted anything like that since the old country. The only trouble was that when he slobbered some it burned a hole in his shirt.

Of all these, however, none could measure up to Alphonse LeBlanc for a real shipyard background. For as many years as he lived here, Alphonse solemnly boasted to all who would listen that, "Me fadder was a band saw and me mudder was a broad-axe!"

Times were not always prosperous in the Essex shipyards. Building followed the ups and downs of the nation's economic cycles. Essex men always managed to keep busy doing something. If nothing better they could always go clamming since it somehow seemed that when they were most needed the clams were most abundant. A shipyard man could usually find humor in his situation though. He might say to a friend, "I think I'll have a Newfoundland sandwich for dinner today." "You don't say. What's a Newfoundland sandwich?" "Why, a couple of herrin' between two stove covers!" "Well, what will you have for dessert?" "This noon I'm having wind puddin' with cobweb sauce." "If all that don't agree with you, what will you take for it?" "I think some spirits of nitre with 'rhubub bitters" should do the trick."

If our friend was asked, "What are you goin' to do today?" the correct answer was, "I'm goin' to pile up what I done yesterday."

The coming of the first cold snap in the fall inevitably prompted the remark, "summer's gone and winter draw (ers) on." To this, somebody was bound to answer, "Yes, it's time to put on the woollen suspenders and fur eye-glasses". There were little anecdotes or riddles that never failed to amuse a new generation of youngsters playing their "putty-can bands" around the shipyard. Such were:

"Oakum and cotton (caulking cotton) had a race and white lead"
or
"Tar, pitch and turpentine—all begins with "a""
or
"I've got a musical horse—he has his corn-et."

The amusement of the young listeners was ample reward to him who told the story.

Humor was where you found it. They laughed at Zeno Andrews who would come to work in the winter wearing so many coats and sweaters that his arms stuck straight out from his sides. However, he fell off the high stage one day and onlookers swear he bounced like a rubber ball He wasn't hurt a bit.

I must speak of Michael Fitzgerald who lived and worked around Essex for many years and who later worked for Mr. Norman Abbott of the ship repair yard in Gloucester. Mike was occasionally sent around the city on errands for the yard and sometimes would do a few for himself while he was at it. Mr. Abbott got wind of it and called Mike into the office one day.

"Say Mike, what's this I hear about you getting a haircut on my time?"

"Why not, Mr. Abbott? It grows on your time."

"Yes, Mike, I know, but it doesn't do all its growing on my time."

"Well, Mr. Abbott, I didn't have it all cut off!"

In the same class was Billy Bagwell who worked for my father for many years. Billy was not one to work too hard if he didn't have to and one day father said to him, "You know, Billy, I wish you'd keep busy. It takes half my time to watch you." "That's nothing, Arthur. It takes all my time watchin' you!"

Then there was the time when Owen Lantz, peering down into the dark depths of the hold called out, "How many of you fellows are down there?" "Five of us, Owen." "Good—I want half of you to come and go with me."

A chance remark or reply could stick with a man for the rest of his career. Father asked Newt Farnham one day to start painting on a certain vessel. "Why sure", said Newt. "Just tell me the color, Arthur, and I'll slap it."

Mose Bushey had borrowed some money in anticipation of his pay envelope and Father, not remembering exactly, asked him the following Saturday: "Let's see Mose, didn't you borrow a dollar from me this week?" "Oh no, Mr. Story, not a dollar, all I borrowed was a half and two quarters."

It must not be assumed that shipyard life was a continual round of comic relief for such was certainly not the case. The hard work was too often interrupted by tragedy and misfortune. Even death occasionally paid a visit to the yards. We read among the records of poor Ed Reynolds who fell overboard and drowned while attempting to row across the river with a line from a newly launched vessel. Or there was Leonard MacKenzie, partner in the firm of James and MacKenzie, who was killed when a piece of lumber fell and struck him on the head. Other men have been killed as a result of falls from staging and one man, when he stepped backward into an open hatchway, perished in the hold far below.

Injuries were common. The four-fingered hand was almost a badge of the ship carpenter, and in those early years no workman's compensation insurance was there to ease the blow. Caulkers could usually be sure that after twenty years or so deafness would over take them. Peter Hubbard once had a long auger enter his leg just below the knee and come out again right above his ankle.

Many men have carried on their work when overtaken by disease they knew was killing them. What else could one do with a family to support? Consider poor Epes Story, forced to go about his work with a cancer on his face and to endure the additional soul-searing burden of a nickname like "No-nosed Epes". How many of us there are who have no conception of what real trial is.

The shipbuilder himself was beset with many particular misfortunes of his own. Oftentimes a boat about to launch would stick to the ways and no amount of pulling with the tug or jacking from shore would start her. Then nothing to do but dismantle the ways and launching cradle and grease them all over again. Worse yet was the heavy vessel that fell over in launching. Sometimes a ways would break and a vessel would fetch up half ashore and half in the water. Needless to say, the expense of getting out of messes like these was considerable. Of course even misfortune can have its lighter view, as when Mr. Oliver Burnham launched one of his boats. She went into the water all right, but with no lines to check, she proceeded to coast across the basin and punch her stern through the back of the grist mill on the opposite bank.

The financial one is always an interesting aspect of any endeavor. In the case of Essex shipbuilders, it is interesting in that of all the scores of men who went into the business, hardly any ever made any money at it. In fact the great majority of Essex ship builders were much the worse, financially, for all their pains. The list of builders who "failed up" as they used to say, is long, not only in Essex but in a great many places where vessels were built. As the old saying goes, "Things are not always what they seem." The classic example was Aaron Burnham who, as the story goes, contracted for and built 22 vessels in 22 months, only to go broke.

I am reminded of "Wash" Tarr who sighed as he watched a new vessel glide down the ways. "She's a beauty, but we didn't make any money on her." Ed Hobbs, who was standing nearby answered, "Well, you must have had a hell of a pile of money when you started because you say that every time a vessel launches!" The remark, sadly, was more truth than fiction, for in the great majority of cases the builder got little more than wages from the business and frequently was deprived of these either through his own lack of business ability or because, all too often, the new vessel was never wholly paid for. Occasionally, of course, a good contract came along that paid well and the builder could put some thing aside. Then along would come another two or three bad ones and away it would all go. My father, who was one of the few successful builders, was in business for nearly sixty years and built well over 400 vessels, yet he made what money he had in the last 15 years of his career. Other men were fortunate enough to have a little money when they started the game, only to see it go down the drain along with the business. I guess the poets were right when they spoke of shipbuilding as "a labor of love."

three

The Skills

IN AMERICA THE PRINCIPAL KIND of wood in wooden ships is, and always has been oak, and oak is among the heaviest of woods. Since everything was done by hand, the work itself in the shipyards was, therefore, extremely heavy and hard. The timbers making up the backbone and frames of a ship were "beat out", as the expression went, with broadaxes and adzes. It took rugged constitutions and arms and backs of iron to do this and to stand it for ten hours a day, six days a week, as they did for a great many years in the early decades of the nineteenth century. No wonder they stopped twice a day for a mug-up of good old New England rum. The cry "Grog-O" coming up in the middle of the forenoon and again in the afternoon must have been music to the ears of tired and sweating souls as they swung those great axes or struggled up a long brow or ramp under the crushing burden of a mighty oaken deck beam.

In the year 1901 there was launched, from the two major yards doing business at the time, a total of thirty vessels having a combined gross tonnage of 3501 or an average of about 117 tons per vessel. Those were not exactly small boats and yet one came down the ways on an average of every twelve days. Bear in mind that in all probability no two of those boats were exactly alike and moreover only a few were built from the same model. Furthermore, the time books for A.D. Story's yard, one of the two in question, and from which eighteen of the vessels came, shows that only about sixty men at any one time were employed by him in that year. To read these records of the Essex shipyards, and particularly to peruse the yearly lists of completed vessels, is to be impressed by what must have been the tremendous amount of work those men did. One wonders how a relatively small number of men doing almost everything by hand could accomplish so much. To cite an example, Mr. A.D. Story, together with Mr. John P. Story and three other men, went down to their yard at 4 A.M. one August morning in 1899 and proceeded to launch the schooner *John J. Flaherty*, a vessel of 162-gross tons. A tug had waited in the river all night for her and by 9 A.M. the vessel had arrived in Gloucester and had her spars all stepped. This same *John J. Flaherty* had been completed in one month following the erection of her frames.

Yet quicker than this was the construction of the schooner *Iceland* in 1892. This 139-gross-ton ship was completed in six weeks, start to finish. The man who had her built had just lost his vessel and needed another in a hurry.

It may have been, however, that the speed record for vessel construction was set back in 1835 when Mr. Parker Burnham built the 55 ton pinky schooner *July*. She was so named after the month it took to complete her. Parenthetically, this same Mr. Parker Burnham distinguished himself by becoming the first Essex shipbuilder to discontinue the serving of rum to the men. He had observed the increasing degree of relish with which one of his young apprentices was consuming his rum and concluded that here indeed was a sorry spectacle and one in which he had no desire to play a part. He therefore gathered his men and proposed that if they would give up the rum, he would serve hot coffee in its place and would add the cost of the rum to their wages. History tells us that the vote to accept was unanimous.

It would appear that while these things were in no sense an example of mass production such as we know today, a remarkable system of building had come about, one which even by present standards must have been extraordinarily efficient. The secret of all this, I think, lay in the fact that most of the men were specialists in some particular phase of the work. It is interesting to examine principal ship carpentering jobs and recall some of the characters who performed them.

If order of a sort is to apply to any such listing, first place must go to the loftsman. This was the man who in the early years often initiated new designs and who could take a model and develop from it the lines and patterns (called molds) by or from which the actual parts were cut. I might say that most early shipbuilders in America possessed little real technical knowledge regarding the finer points of naval architecture. The shapes of boats were evolved pretty much from the experience of those who sailed and built them, and were achieved by the simple method of carving a scale model from a large wooden block made of several layers. When the model was done to the satisfaction of those concerned, it was taken apart and the layers or sections were traced out on paper. It was here that the loftsman's job began, for he took the small scale lines and enlarged them to full size upon the floor of his loft, proceeding in turn to make from these his "molds" of every piece, hence the name "mold-loft".

The last mold loft in Essex—I can remember it well—was owned by Mr. Archer B. Poland. It was a T-shaped building, not very large, over on School Street, South Essex. Mr. Poland was in business for himself and contracted to make molds for all the yards in Essex. As a boy I loved to go into this place with my father when he went over occasionally to inquire after the progress of a new vessel. Mr. Poland would be padding around the paper covered floor in his carpet slippers picking his way among what seemed like a small forest of awls stuck in the floor to hold in place the long battens used to draw out the waterlines and sections. Ranged around the perimeter of the room were dusty benches on which were scattered an awesome array of hand tools of every description, miscellaneous chunks of wood, pieces of patterns or what-have-you in the most satisfying sort of casual disorder. Overhead in cob-webby storage were ladders, baskets, fruit pickers, still more patterns and other odd items hung up for future reference or occasional use. It was altogether a most enchanting place. I can even remember how it smelled, an interesting combination of the musty, dusty objects, mingled with pine shavings and the heavy gray paper.

Possessed as he was of considerable specialized ability, Mr. Poland was inclined to be rather secretive about his talent and designs and would go to some trouble to cover over lines on his floor if he felt a prospective caller might turn out to be a little inquisitive. People have remarked they could hear boards slapping down all over the place as they walked up the driveway to the shop door. By the time they got in, there wasn't much that anyone could see. Mr. Poland was a true craftsman, however, and lofted hundreds of boats in his lifetime.

The molds, once they reached the yard, were taken by the man who molded the timber and were used in the selection and marking of the stock to be cut. This job consisted of rolling over the pieces in a pile of new timber and tracing out the shape of the frames prior to cutting. Any one frame was made up of several pieces and these had to be carefully selected from the available stock and correctly marked so that the finished frame stood in proper relationship to the ones adjoining it. There were many tricks to this trade, but it was especially important to utilize the timber to its best advantage making use of natural curves of the

Mr. Archer B. Poland at work in his mold loft. Note the carpet slippers.

wood where possible, yet avoiding bad knots or rotten spots and still leave as little waste as possible. This last, incidentally, could make considerable difference in the yard's profit margin over a period of time since trimmings and leftovers were good for nothing but firewood.

A good molder, having gotten the knack of the job, could do pretty well for himself since the job was often on a piecework basis. Mr. John Prince Story, who at 85 was still doing it, told me he was paid $1.00 per frame for molding and at one time was molding frames for two different boats in two different yards at the same time. After molding six frames a day he would quit and go home, fearing the rest of the gang would be mad at his making so much money.

John Prince, as he was universally known, was a keen man serving as foreman for Mr. John Bishop at his yard in Gloucester and later for many years as foreman for the James yard in Essex. He never missed a trick. Once a stem piece for a new boat turned out a large black knot down near the keel. John was about to have it cut out and a graving piece put in when, out of the corner of his eye, he caught sight of the captain just getting off the trolley car from Gloucester. Quick as a wink John doffed his coat and hung it on a handy nail, neatly covering the knot.

This scene appears in the Town Seal of Essex. The *William H. Rider* is on the ways at the yard of John Prince Story. In the river is the water boat *Lillian Russell*.

He was too late, though, the captain must have seen him do it because he made a beeline for the coat. The whole stem piece came out.

As sometimes happened, vessels would go out of shape during construction, especially during the spring when the frost was coming out of the ground. This would raise or lower the supporting shores and the vessel, as a result, might be perhaps a little wider on one side than the other. A captain discovered this once and called to John to ask how it happened.

"Well," said John, "I'll tell you. See those cows in the pasture over there? Well, last week they got out one night and came over here. By the time morning came they'd knocked out half the shores under this vessel and that's what made her twist."

John's house was just a few doors up the street from my Aunt Julia's. Aunt Julie, as everyone called her, was a year older than John. In fact, she lived to be 102 and her birthdays came to be noteworthy events. Although John and she had, in a sense, grown up together and had always been friendly neighbors, he rarely ever called in to see her except on her birthday when he would generally put in an appearance. Once, when she was celebrating her 98th, she said to him, "John, why don't you stop in and see me more often? You only come in on my birthday."

"Oh, Julie," he said. "I couldn't." "Why not?" she queried. "Well," said John, "I'm afraid people might talk!" John Prince was in business for himself as a shipbuilder at two periods in his lifetime. This is not especially remarkable in itself except that a period of forty-seven years intervened, and his last and really extensive effort began in 1941 when he was approximately 81 years old. Working with his grandson from 1941 to 1945, he built seven large vessels, supervising all operations and molding his own timber. He was the last of a great race of Essex shipbuilders, and, at 98, was still living alone in his house on Winthrop Street. He would go down to the Post Office nearly every day where he met his old friend Tom Boutchie, who himself was 94. Together they would spend a while observing the passing scene and commenting philosophically upon modern folk-ways. Said John one day, "What they can't do with gasoline, don't get done these days!" On another occasion as they talked, Tom remarked, "You know John, it ain't the high cost of livin' that hurts. It's the cost of high livin'!"

John worked with my father, A.D. Story, for a time during which he subcontracted the labor to build three similar small schooners. In each case Father furnished all materials and John furnished the labor to build the hull complete except for joiner work in cabin and forecastle. John's price for the first one was $900. Since that proved to be not quite enough, he charged $950 for each of the other two. These little schooners were about 80 feet long on deck and on the basis of John's figure, the completed cost of each must have been in the neighborhood of $2,500.

Besides his work in the shipyards, John Prince served the Town of Essex for many years as one of the board of selectmen. His reputation for economy still lingers. He also, on one occasion, helped conduct a memorable episode in law enforcement. It seems that the selectmen hadn't been having much luck getting their chief of police to break up a card game which had been going on for some time in an old shop, formerly part of Lantz's shipyard. The board eventually decided that if they wanted it stopped they'd have to go and do it themselves, so over they went to stage a raid. Peeking through a window, they could see that the boys were in there all right, sitting just beyond the pool table that stood opposite the door. Concluding that the door must be securely bolted, the selectmen decided they would all three rush it at once and break it down, creating as they did so a considerable element of surprise. They backed off and gave a mighty rush. The door, however, was not securely fastened, and flew open at a touch, catapulting the board of selectmen into a tangled heap underneath the pool table. Before they could extricate themselves, the last of the poker players was just disappearing out the side window.

Several years ago I invited John to go with me to see another old ship carpenter with whom he used to work and who was then unable to get around much. His reply was, "I know what he wants! He just wants to talk about old times. You can't live in the past; you've got to look ahead." That from a man approaching 100 years of age.

Another man who did a good deal of molding was my Uncle Eddie, or more properly, Edwin J. Story, one of Father's younger brothers. I loved to sit on the piles of timber talking to Uncle Eddie and watching him as he worked. I particularly enjoyed his whistled renditions of *The Whistler and his Dog*. As a matter of fact, Uncle Eddie's real love was music and he was an accomplished player of both the clarinet and the oboe. He much preferred to work as a musician and did so whenever the opportunity arose. For several seasons he was a regular member of Barnum and Bailey's circus band travelling all over the country. In the winter months he played in the orchestras of several of the Boston theatres.

As a younger man Uncle Eddie always rode a motorcycle, but following a bad spill he abandoned this vehicle in favor of a bicycle which he rode until he was quite an old man.

More than these things the town of Essex is indebted to Uncle Eddie for his photography. He was one of the town's pioneer photographers and, with his great sense of history, did much to preserve a pictorial record of the life and particularly the shipyards of the town.

Returning to our story of the shipyard men and their work, we have seen how the parts were marked out on the pieces of timber. From now on it was a question of cutting and putting them together. Until the advent of the steam band saw in the middle 1880's the cutting out fell to the hewers who, as I said, "beat out" the timbers and frames with their broadaxes. These men could split a pencil line with a broadaxe and think nothing of it. The finished surface would look and feel as though it had been planed.

Other men operated the pit saw or "whip saw" as it was some times called. This was the means of sawing the long planks that formed the outside and inside skins of the ship. A whip saw consisted of a narrow blade about 4 or 5 feet long held in a rectangular wooden framework. The ends of the frame were the handles by which the saw was pulled up and down. A plank was laid on some supporting pieces over a pit or depression in the ground. With one man in the pit underneath and another man on top, the saw was pulled up and down until the cut was made. This was work of the most rugged kind, especially if the plank was 50 or 60 feet long, as they often were, and 2 or 3 inches thick. Imagine the lost soul in that pit on a day when it was 95 in the shade getting a face full of sawdust on every down

Steve Price hews on timber for a "stern circle."

stroke! It was frequently the boys just starting out who got this job and an old-timer on the top could make it brutal for the youngster if he felt inclined.

A trade with a curious sounding name to present day ears was that of the dubber. A dubber was a man who went along ahead of the plankers and trimmed off the heavy frames with his adze in order that the planks, as they were put on, would lie fairly and firmly against the frames. One strip of plank around a vessel's hull is known as a "streak" and a good planking gang would some times put on two streaks of plank in a day. This meant that all the frames in that boat had to be trimmed twice in that day, once for each streak. That's a lot of chopping. Moreover, much of it was overhead and on frames that sometimes were 14 or 16 inches wide. If the dubber couldn't keep ahead of his plankers the whole job had to slow down or wait for him and that, of course, was bad. Among the shipwrights it was an important job. If the dubber didn't trim his frames properly the planks would not lie "fair" and he would have to go back and do a place over again. Men like Charlie Madden, old John Hubbard and Leander Doucette are still remembered for the way they could dub.

One of the greatest dubbers from the standpoint of work produced was John Wetmore. It was John's custom to take a contract for the dubbing of a vessel and he has been known to dub two vessels at the same time. He would dub off a streak on one vessel, rush over to the other to dub another streak and then again to the first. More than that, the two vessels would sometimes be in different yards. Men who remembered have told of seeing him run from one yard to another to keep ahead of his plankers.

Such strenuous effort did not always leave proper time to grind his adze. He would bang away with the thing getting duller and duller until out of sheer desperation or exhaustion he had to stop. My father once sat watching him do this as he dubbed on a boat building in Father's yard and concluded he would have to make John sharpen that adze. It was almost twelve o'clock and as soon as John dropped his adze on the stage and went to dinner, Father took it and finding a large rock in the weeds nearby gave the adze a few healthy belts on the edge of the blade. The he put it back where he had found it. Upon coming back from dinner John picked up his adze and eyeing it ruefully he disappeared to the grindstone where he remained the rest of the afternoon grinding out those awful nicks. He took more pains with his adze after that.

It is interesting to observe that in later years, with the introduction to wooden shipyards of a certain amount of machinery and electric power tools, the speed, volume and quality of the work has never equaled that turned out by the old fellows who did everything by hand. They were good mechanics and took pride in their work and the vessels they were building. Every man understood what he was doing and its relationship to the whole job. The foreman found it necessary to tell a man only once what he wanted done and then concern himself no further until that job was finished.

Perhaps we did achieve, without regarding it as such, a rather high degree of mass production. The presence within a single general trade of so many regularly practiced skills must have been the answer to the ability to produce so many ships in a short time. I have spoken of a few of these skills. There were many more. Some fellows did nothing but bore holes for the fastenings using long augers to which steel cranks were welded. Planks were fastened to the frames with locust tree nails, better known as trunnels. Those were 1 1/8 or 1 1/4 inches in diameter and each had to have a hole bored for it. There were thousands in any one vessel, some of them through as much as 14 inches of solid oak. For doing this job a man got one cent per hole. Skill in this case was more a question of muscle for the stronger the arms and the greater the endurance the more holes a man could bore and therefore the more he made. Good borers made up to five dollars a day.

The men are fastening off a "streak" of plank. John Hubbard (left) dubs for the next "streak." John Conrad drives "trunnels" and Robert D'Entremont bores holes for "trunnels."

Caulkers were a breed all by themselves. A rough, tough crowd they usually were whose services were in demand wherever wooden ships were built or repaired. A caulker's job, essentially, was to drive the seams or other joints in the hull's outer surface full of cotton and oakum to make the ship watertight. Usually they were men who learned the trade while quite young and proceeded to follow it all their lives. They customarily worked in pairs or small groups keeping mostly to themselves, yet maintaining a running feud with the carpenters. If a new boat after launching was nice and tight, the caulkers had done a good job of caulking. If she leaked, the carpenters had done a poor job searching for imperfections.

Caulkers speak a sort of language of their own and have special sets of implements for doing their work. For example, there are many types of irons for doing the actual caulking. Some were wide and thick for large seams, others narrow and thin for small tight seams. Others were specially shaped for inaccessible places or particular circumstances. Some were made especially for making sea wider if they were too tight. These were called dumb irons. Some were made to push the oakum way in after first driving with the lighter tools. These were called hawsing irons or making irons.

A caulker's principal tool was his wooden mallet which he cherished as he would an infant son. A caulking mallet was T- shaped with a stout handle about a foot long and a head about 15 inches long when new, and whose ends were approximately 1½ inches in diameter. About each end of the head was a steel ring to keep it from flaying out in use. Both ends of the head are used alternately so that the wear on each is uniform. A mallet from black mesquite was a caulker's first choice, with live oak perhaps second.

Oakum, which is a form of tarred hemp, comes in tightly bound bales, which are made up in turn of smaller bundles or balls. Before oakum can be driven, the balls must be opened up and the long continuous strands pulled out and stretched, or spun, and then wound again into smaller usable balls. It is interesting to note in passing that the caulkers used oakum for bandages, believing it was antiseptic and beneficial, and also preferred it to old catalogues in the little house behind the sawmill.

Every yard had a small building or perhaps a room of the larger shop where oakum was stored and where the caulkers went to spin oakum on stormy days or when they were caught up in their work. Such a place was referred to as the oakum loft. They were wonderful places, and made an impression on my youthful consciousness that I can never forget. The one in Father's yard was a small wooden building which had once been somebody's little boathouse. It stood up on the hillside at the rear of the yard where the timber was kept. Sand served to insulate the hot stove from the floor and made a convenient place for the men to spit their tobacco juice. There were windows in only one side, as I remember. On the other side were overturned kegs with burlap "cushions" used for seats and some slanting boards for backrests. On the walls were a collection of pictures of the great schooners and a gallery of the old-time bare-knuckle pugilists, prominent among them being the Boston strong boy, John L. Sullivan. When the weather was cold or otherwise unfit to work outside, the caulkers would be in here seated on their kegs with a leather apron over one knee. A ball of new oakum would be on the floor beside them while they pulled the flattened strand over the aproned knee. As they did so they would stretch it out and roll it a couple of times with the palm of their hand on the leather to give the oakum a usable consistency. The air was blue with smoke and oaths as they spun their yarns as well as the oakum. I was always a little afraid of this place, realizing that it was just a bit out of bounds for a small boy. The sight and particularly the smell of the place, a veritable symphony of stinks, will never leave me.

Mr. Eric Sloane of Connecticut, in one of his books, speaks about "sounds" as distinct from "noises". I know just what he means. The cry "Frame-up" was a part of our lives in Essex and so, perhaps more than anything else, was the ring of the caulker's mallet. This sound is unduplicated by anything else in the realm of nature and man. The blow of a hammer hitting a spike or a piece of wood falling to the stage is a noise, but the caulking mallet striking against its iron creates a piercing, ringing sound which carries for a great distance and lets the world know that something is going on, that work is being accomplished, that ships are taking form.

How unfortunate it is that we must so often wait until something is gone before appreciating it or even being aware of it. Generations of Essex people were born, lived and died amid the sounds of the shipyards: the caulking mallets, the sound of axe and ache ringing against white oak, the millions of hammer blows, and the shouts of the men. At the time it was a part of their existence, like the air they breathed. Now that it is all gone we realize what a satisfying chorus it was and how silent the town is now.

When the rough construction of the hull was largely done, when the ship carpenters were through and the hull was caulked, the finish men took over to complete the job. Some smoothed up the outside while others built forecastles and cabins. Smoothing, called outboard joinering, involved going over the whole of the out side of the hull with hand planes and scrapers. Planks were planed lengthwise and then crosswise (called traversing) and finally hand scraped until they shone. As in other operations, this was also frequently done on a contract basis with a team of men working from yard to yard. Peter Hubbard and John Doyle worked together as outboard joiners for many years and smoothed countless boats. Besides smoothing the boats they smoothed many rough edges from long days of hard shipyard work for both men were full of wit and fun and enjoyed a good joke even if it was on them. John, universally known as Skeet, could find some humor in just about any situation. He was quite a ballplayer in his younger days, and evening down town was a member of the noted Hayscales Quartet.

Peter was a little Nova Scotian who was always into something. His compatriots called him "leetle one" and said he was so short he needed a stage to plane the deck. He played ball, too, and won undying fame by leaping into the creek out in center field to snag a long fly ball which otherwise would have gone for a home run. He and his father won a Fourth of July rowing race on the river by secretly smearing the bottom of their dory with grease. They outdistanced the field with no trouble at all. He built several little boats of his own, in one of which he rigged an old bicycle frame geared to a set of paddles. By sitting on the bicycle seat and turning the pedals, she went along at a great clip.

Pete was game for anything, whether sports or a round of cards. He would even shoot a little crap if the occasion warranted. He went into the Twentieth Century Club one night to find a lively group rolling the dice. Penniless at the moment, he cast about for some way to join in, when what should catch his eye but a lone dime winking from the bottom of a spittoon. With this as a grubstake, he pitched in with the gang and before the evening was out marched triumphantly home bearing $90 in his pocket.

During an interlude away from the shipyards he once worked as a house carpenter for Pod Burnham at Conomo Point. Pod gave him some shingles to put on the side of a cottage while he went up town for more stock. Peter, determined to make a good showing, nailed the shingles on at a furious rate. At length the boss re turned and Peter, glancing up, said, "There, Pod, ain't I loose?"

"You're loose, all right," said Pod. "You loosen up every damn one and put 'em on the right way!"

When Peter hired a vacant cottage that winter at Conomo Point for his honeymoon, the boys couldn't resist it. They went down beforehand and stuffed the chimney full of old bags and then sat back to wait for the inevitable result.

Peter had an indomitable spirit. He would try anything. No project was too tough for him to conquer somehow. He once got a job to repair the hull of a 28-foot motorboat. The boat was in Annisquam at the time and Pete wanted to bring it home to make it handier to work on. So bring it home he did—by rowing the thing alone across three miles of Ipswich Bay and then another mile and a half into the Essex River. Here, with the tide racing out through the narrows, he almost gave up until somebody in a motor launch threw him a line and towed him the rest of the way.

"How did you feel, Pete?" they asked him.

"I felt like a lone smelt in the Bay of Fundy," said Pete.

I can't leave the subject of outboard joinering without paying a brief word of tribute to Alan Bruton, outboard joiner in the James yard. Bruton had a couple of idiosyncrasies which had best not be mentioned here, but will be long remembered for his reply to the visitor who loudly boasted of his experiences as a sailor. After listening to him for a while Bruton said in disgust, "Mister, I've wrung more water out of my mittens than you ever sailed over!"

The aristocrats among the ship carpenters were the inboard joiners, the men who built the living quarters into the ships and the structures on deck. A good inboard joiner is one of the world's finest mechanics since his work encompasses everything from rough carpentry to the most delicate of cabinetwork. An inboard joiners' work is complicated aboard ship by the fact that the spaces in which he must work and the objects he must build are neither straight, level or plumb. Good house carpenters are lost when put into a vessel to work, but the inboard joiner, after being brought up to ship work, could do house carpentering with one hand tied behind him.

Even in a field such as this, where ability in any phase was taken for granted, the work fell into patterns with some men specializing in forecastles and others in cabins and deckhouses. Forecastles are in the forward end of a ship and generally contain the crew's living quarters. Here are most of the bunks, the galley and ice chest.

When I was a boy, the man who built most of the forecastles for Father was Jack Doyle. He was a rough and ready Irishman with a glint of the old sod in his eye and a tremendous capacity for work and chewing tobacco. His cheek stuck out in a perpetual hump and the pile of chips he made as he worked was dripping with tobacco juice most of the time. He could turn out as much work in a day as two ordinary men and usually did.

At the other end of the ship, building the cabin trunk and quarters for the captain was Ed Perkins, one of the greatest ship carpenters who ever lived. He was a master craftsman in every sense of the word. As a young man he started in with his father building cabins and forecastles. He learned the trade in the old fashioned way, taking pains to observe the old maxim that "anything worth doing is worth doing well." It is he, I believe, who was credited with the observation, "When you hear a man say, 'There, that's good enough', you can make up your mind it's a damn poor job!"

I suppose it was the case in other localities, but certainly in Essex it was customary for the carpenters and ship joiners to have their own shops. Some like Mr. Perkins' or Frank Cogswell's, a little way down the street, were beautifully built two story buildings and were matters of considerable pride to the owner. They were used in getting out stock for a job or for making small parts of the finish work on the vessels such as companionways, sky lights, panel doors, shutters, tables, etc. Often a ship joiner in his off times turned out items of beautiful furniture in his shop.

Standing in his back yard, Mr. Perkins' shop is today a veritable museum. To step through the door is to step back 75 years to the days when to be a carpenter meant more than owning a hammer and saw and holding a union card. Preserved just as he used them are all the old tools and implements employed by the ship joiners of generations ago. It's easy to see where the term or name joiner came from. When Mr. Perkins joined together two pieces of wood the joint appeared as one. He made many of his tools himself, particularly the planes of which there must be over a hundred around the shop. Hung up or standing around are odds and ends of boards or moldings, pieces of furniture, cabinets, chests of drawers, more tools and a mingling of old ads, pictures and clippings. Nowhere today would there be a building quite like this. Wealthy collectors have spent huge sums to recreate artificially a shop like Mr. Perkins'.

He had a great sense of history and took the trouble to make note of events both local and national as they occurred. He always kept clippings, pictures and notices of interest especially about the shipyards and kept a record of the jobs he did. He had the curious habit of making notes upon the walls or beams of the shop, particularly the dates of death of men who were well known in town.

I have spent many pleasant hours with Mr. Perkins in his living room listening to his recollections of the old days in the shipyards. At 96 he was one of the last links with a remarkable past. His memory for scenes and events was almost photographic and stretched back to his earliest boyhood. He took great interest in all that went on, often traveling considerable distance to see the things about which he had heard or read. He liked to take a ride on the boats he had helped to build and would sometimes travel over to Gloucester on the new boats as they were towed out of the river to their home port. I recall his story of how as a young boy many years ago he sailed out of the river on a new boat built in the yard of Mr. Oliver Burnham. It must have been before the days of towing out the new boats with a steam tug, for this boat was fully rigged with all canvas set. Mr. Burnham himself acted as temporary captain and was dressed in his Sunday best, even to the point of wearing a magnificent tall beaver hat. A sudden fresh breeze struck the boat as she passed out of the river into the bay and before sail could be shortened, she was nearly hove down on her beam ends with crew and passengers sliding down the deck into the lee scuppers. Mr. Burnham never lost his composure nor his beaver hat, but bracing his feet against the slanting deck he clung manfully to the wheel while shouting his orders. Through squall and confusion that beaver hat stood triumphantly in its place.

Somewhat after the fashion of the pastry cook whose job in the bakery consists of applying the icing to the cakes, were the men of the shipyard whose work was to apply the decorative trim: the name boards, the trail boards, and the ornamental carvings. This indeed was a rare and delicate skill and its practitioners were (and are) held in the highest regard. As might be imagined, there were very few who could do this, but those who did have the talent turned out some of the finest examples of hand craftsmanship, carving and design known to America. Their work had a quality of grace and rhythm seldom seen in other crafts and a ship lent itself admirably to the expression of such art.

In Essex the decorative work on the ships was largely confined to the trailboard and forward nameboards. (A trailboard was the narrow and sweeping little panel that curved up under the bowsprit at the peak of the ship's bow.) Sometimes the names on the stern were also embellished with a little carving. I have never heard that our vessels were given figureheads and I never knew of anyone in town who carved them. It was the custom here to affix nameboards with the letters deeply and beautifully etched, preceded and followed by long, tapering scrollwork. In the days of the clipper-bowed vessels a set of trailboards was placed under the bowsprit, and later when spoon-bowed vessels came along, the scrolls were carved around the hawse-pipes. It was the almost universal practice to finish off names and scroll work in gold leaf.

One of the greatest exponents of this art in Essex shipbuilding was Mr. John Cummings Choate, more commonly known simply as John Cummings. There are but few examples of his work extant but such as there are revealing an artistry of the highest order. There are, however, some of the patterns that he originated and luckily there are many historical photographs, which show the names, and carvings he made.

Another who did this work and a man whom I can remember was Mr. John Finlayson. Johnny Finn, as everyone called him, was a huge man who must have weighed 300 lbs. but he had a fine artistic eye and lettered a great many boats. He once made me a lovely little model sailboat, which I prized for many years. I remember that it had a gear wheel from an old alarm clock for a steering wheel, and the mast was surmounted by a tiny bright red glass bead.

The last Essex man to do any of the decorative work was my distant cousin, Mr. Lewis H. Story. His father was Newton Story, so everyone called Lewis, Looie Newt, or sometimes just Lou.

Lou was a quiet, gentle soul who never married and who lived in the old family homestead for most of his life with one or the other of his two sisters. He worked off and on at various jobs in the shipyard, becoming, in late years, a name man and finally a loftsman. He had very bushy black eyebrows and always carried a little basket over one arm when he walked down the street.

In the last years of his life there was little employment for him in the shipyards, and to eke out a meager existence he turned to the carving of decorative plaques which people would buy as wedding gifts, etc. They were fine hand-painted bas-reliefs depicting an Essex schooner under full sail. He sometimes made models of the schooners or the famous clipper ships.

As a young man Lou cultivated an intense interest in the history of sailing ships and more especially in the compiling of records of Essex shipbuilding. It reached the point where his whole life's interest was wrapped up in the accumulation of these records and he spent literally years in their preparation. He combed every known source for his information and came to be an authority on Essex boats consulted by scholars and museums. He eventually reduced his material to a large card index that he kept in two shoeboxes. Every night when he went to bed, the shoeboxes rested on a chair beside him. If the house caught fire he was determined to save his records. Nothing else really mattered to Lou. His precious shoe boxes, I am happy to say, are now the property of The Peabody Museum of Salem where they will be properly kept and made available for study. This writer, the Town of Essex, and any who are, or will be, interested in the factual records of Essex shipbuilding owe a tremendous debt of gratitude to Lewis H. Story for his devotion to preserving the story of a great heritage.

So we see that a vessel was constructed by the application of a large number of skills that, in their turn, were merely reflecting the personalities of the men who possessed them. The poet might say that the projection of all these personalities was the creation of the personality and character of the ship. Certainly, and I know this from personal experience, the men who built our ships had more than a passing interest and affection for their labors and when a ship slid down the ways she took with her something of each man who had helped to build her. Does a ship have a soul? Maybe so, maybe not.

four

Around the Town

I WOULD ALMOST BE WILLING to wager that the Town of Essex has about as many subdivisions as does the city of New York. First of all, the Essex River divides the town into its two major parts, Essex and South Essex. Actually both might well be towns by themselves and each one does have its own post office, but there is, and always has been, only one Town government. However, Essex is further divided into Essex Center, Essex Falls, Lakeville, Gregory Island, Loggin's Cove, Tubtown, North End and Hog Island. South Essex divides into Thompson Island, Burnham's Corner, Clay Point, Rocky Hill, East District and Conomo Point with Conomo Point having a Conomo Village, Lufkin's Point and Robbins Island. All these in a town roughly five miles by three miles.

Before passing, I might say that Tubtown got its name from the time some sports from Essex Falls decided to have some fun and went up to Pond Street near the lake one night and climbed up on the roof of a little house where prayer meeting was going on. After making sure nobody heard them, they gingerly set a washtub over the chimney and beat a stealthy retreat. The story goes that prayer meeting came to a choking halt but the incident gave the locality a new name.

In spite of unity in government there has always been a vague feeling of rivalry between Essex and South Essex. This rivalry was fanned into flame when, in 1893, the town got ready to build its new town hall. The ruckus, stirred up by the choice of sites for the new edifice, was something many still remember. In the end it was built in Essex Center, but the town meeting held to decide the issue has never been equaled for intensity of feeling, excitement or partisan support.

Naturally everybody who lived in South Essex wanted the town hall on his side of the river, while Essex folks wanted it on their side. It was informally argued and discussed for months. Every effort was made to get out the vote and meeting night saw the lower floor of the Congregational Church, used until that time as a meeting hall, filled to over-flowing. The atmosphere was tense with excitement when the door opened once more to admit stalwarts from Essex Center supporting between them old Mr. Eveleth, a frail white-whiskered gentleman, leaning on his cane. The leader of the South Essex forces took one look and springing to his feet shouted, "Boys, I guess we're licked. They're bringin' 'em up from the cemetery!"

The final vote gave the town hall to Essex by a very narrow margin and the feelings aroused carried over for many years. The kids especially would take things pretty carefully and put up a brave front when going from one side of town to the other. It was never safe to cross the river without having your gang with you. This gave rise to all sorts of pranks. Once in the night before, the Fourth, a crowd sneaked over to the center from South Essex and, by backing a large high-wheeled wagon under it, swiped the bandstand right out of the square, returning in triumph with it. Selectmen and constables tried to make them bring it back but it never got there.

That town hall, one might say, has divided the population right down to the present day, except that now people argue about whether or not it's handsome. Personally, I think it's the homeliest building I ever saw, combining the ultimate in all the preposterous features of Victorian ugliness. In fact, it's so homely that maybe it does seem handsome in a backhanded sort of way. At least there is probably not another building like it in the whole United States.

The only redeeming feature about the whole affair was that when they finally got around to building it, it didn't cost the town a cent. A man named Burnham provided the money for it in his will. The donor, Mr. Thomas Oliver Hazard Perry Burnham, had been the affluent owner of the famous Old Corner Book Store in Boston, and thereby lies something of a story in itself. Mr. Burnham was born and brought up in Essex and in his later years became an exceedingly prosperous Boston merchant. The time came when a public hall of some sort with space for town offices seemed urgently necessary and various among the town fathers conceived the idea that it would be nice if such a building could be a gift. Somehow they alighted on Mr. Burnham as being one who certainly could and perhaps would do it. Accordingly a town meeting delegated a committee to see Mr. Burnham and put the proposition up to him. A forthright idea, to say the least.

Perhaps because he was too startled by the suddenness of the proposal or maybe because he was taken aback by such an effrontery, Mr. Burnham declined the honor of their invitation. The committee came home and duly reported the results of the conference. The incident appeared to be closed.

Nevertheless, when Mr. Burnham died some time afterwards, a generous section of his will provided Essex with its sought-after town hall and further, a library to go with it.

But homely or not, the old Town Hall has seen some good times and many lively ones, too. The building was completed and dedicated in February of 1894 and the following June witnessed the ceremonies of the first class to graduate from our newly established Essex High School. From then on it became an integral part of the town's civic and social life. Socials, plays, banquets, pageants, dances and church bazaars followed in rapid succession. In fall or winter came the Chautauqua for a three-day stand; in the spring came the town meeting and the minstrel show, and each June a fresh band of hopeful and earnest young seniors sat nervously in starched solemnity on the platform, eager to receive their diplomas from the hands of the school board.

One of the greatest town hall institutions and one, which, surprisingly enough still survives in Essex after nearly 60 years, is the annual minstrel show. Sponsored by a civic organization and put on in the late winter or early spring it is an event for which most of the town turns out. Through the years there have been scores of homefolks who, while never dreaming of appearing on a stage under other circumstances, would don costumes and black face to crack jokes about their fellows and shout the good old minstrel songs.

The black-faced ones sat in the front row on the stage on either side of the interlocutor and were the end men. (Man or woman—they were still end men.) Immediately behind were the soloists, quartets and specialty singers. The job of interlocutor was customarily filled by one of the town's more prominent and popular citizens who usually turned out to be a star in his own right.

The end men, however, were the main part of the show with jokes, dancing and high jinks and especially with the topical songs. A topical song presented a wonderful opportunity for a local poet to shaft his neighbors and townfolk in a good-natured sort of way, spoofing hometown institutions and foibles and touching upon subjects that might not otherwise be politely mentioned. The jokes were no good unless well-known characters around town were used as principals.

For example, Sambo would say to Mr. Bones, "Say, Brother Bones, you know Lyman James was settin' on his front piarza the other day when Gramp Watson came by with a tip-cart load of manure!"

"Izzat so?" says Mr. Bones.

"Yep, and Lyman hollers, 'What you gonna do with that manure?'"

"'Gonna put it on my strawberries' says Gramp."

"You are?" says Lyman. "I usually put sugar and cream on mine!"

The topical songs and jokes were not always taken in a spirit of fun and occasionally the butt of an end man's joke took violent exception to the play upon his good name. I had an uncle who was a partner in a tailoring business with a man named Wetmore, the firm being Wetmore and Story. One night at the show Rastus said:

"Say, Mr. Interlocutor, do you know why Wetmore and Story's suits are like Fitz H. James' wife?"

"No Rastus, I don't. Tell me why."

"Well," said Rastus, "it's because they're Mis'-Fitz!"

Amid the haw-hawing, Mr. Wetmore was out of his seat in a flash and before anyone could stop him, was up on the stage taking a swing at Rastus.

The first Monday in March has traditionally been Town Meeting Day in Essex. In years gone by it was the custom for the men of the town to lay aside their ordinary pursuits and gather in the town hall on the morning of Town Meeting Day, there to begin the task of transacting the town's business for the ensuing year. They began at nine o'clock with the reading and discussion of reports of the various town officers and departments after which they got to the meat of the situation, namely the raising, assessing and appropriating of the funds. At noon they stopped while everybody repaired to the Grand Army Hall where dinner would be served by the ladies of the Women's Relief Corps. After dinner it was back to the business again with more discussion and the election of town officers. If things didn't become too heated the meeting was over by four or half-past.

In that unsophisticated era, a dollar was hard to come by, and before they spent their hard-earned tax money, the town fathers made fairly certain of where it was going and why. Doing this took a considerable amount of talk, not all of it gentle or polite. The old fellows were not afraid to name names or to speak their minds if the occasion demanded—and it often demanded. Speaking of all this brings to mind a curious footnote to the conduct of town business in which many years ago a plan was devised whereby for a time the rights to sell liquor were auctioned off to the highest bidder at each annual meeting.

In the conduct of governmental affairs the practicing of politics has been traditional in America, even down to the community level, and Essex was by no means an exception. Essex men were not above attempting to use public office for a little personal advantage here and there or to take a sporting chance in the election of a particular candidate. We had a prominent man who ran for and was elected to the office of Road Surveyor for the South District in order that he might get the road up to his own farm re-gravelled. In one fell swoop and in a space of one day he spent his appropriation hiring every team in the neighborhood. When called to account at the next town meeting, as he knew he would be, he was quite frank to admit what he'd done. "I've been trying for years to get that job done with no success," he said, "so I guessed I'd run for Surveyor and do it myself!" So saying he sat down and let them nominate somebody else for Surveyor next year.

Back about 1908 or '09 a masterful bit of political acumen was exhibited by Perry (Pod) Burnham in the election of Eddie Willis (Andrews) to the school board. It seems that when it came around to the elections in the meeting of that year the only man who appeared to want the vacancy on the school board was Mr. Bert Cogswell. Mr. Cogswell had tried unsuccessfully for the job in several years past. Now he felt that at last it was to be his year. To this end he had had ballots all printed bearing his name. As nomination time drew near it was whispered around that Eddie Willis, a retired dentist and man about town would also be interested. At once a hurried conference among Pod, Erastus Burnham and Mike Callahan was gathered over in a corner. "Rastus," the proprietor of the local print shop, suggested that if they could get some ballots printed up with their man's name on he might yet make it. Noting the hour as being close to noon, Poddy jumped up and cried, "Mr. Moderator, I think everybody is getting pretty hungry, and I move we adjourn and go to dinner!"

An immediate chorus of ayes carried the motion and while the gang trooped up to the Grand Army Hall for dinner, Poddy, Rastus and Mike hustled down to the shop of Burnham's Job Print and in a twinkling had the type set up for a school committee ballot bearing the name of Eddie Willis. With the meeting resumed and voting about to start, there was the name of our friend Eddie Willis on the ballot. Confronted now with a choice for the job the electorate decided to elect Eddie and thus poor Mr. Cogswell was defeated again. All entreaties and protests to the moderator were to no avail.

Sometimes a man's comments on the doings of his fellows would backfire. Mr. Frank Ellis Burnham, one of the town's leading businessmen, often arose in meeting to complain that he couldn't make much sense out of the town auditors report. Finally the meeting decided that the man for the job was Frank Ellis Burnham and elected him by acclamation to serve for the ensuing year. He was a good sport about it and took the job although discovering to his chagrin that it took quite a high degree of professional ability. At length, and in order to extricate himself from his predicament, he hired a firm of certified public accountants to do the job, paying for it out of his own pocket.

I remember a barber we had once named Ezra Hinkley who, when sober, was a pretty good barber as barbers go, but whose real claim to fame was as a town meeting orator. I don't imagine he ever had much education but what a spellbinder he was when it came to an issue which he felt demanded his attention. He would stride to the front of the hall from his place at the rear where he usually stood, and brandishing his copy of the Town Report, would give it all he had. We had another one, Lyman James, who always wanted to know as he looked at a list of expenditures " - - what this 'miscellaneous' is for." Or there was Luther Burnham who said, in regard to a proposal to install a public water system, that it was a "damnable, perfidious outrage."

Another rivalry, of a sort, existed between the town's fire companies. We had two, one in Essex and the other in South Essex. The Essex engine, smaller of the two, was named the Amazon and the South Essex engine was called Essex No. 2. I hasten to add that the rivalry was a friendly one and the two companies worked together if the occasion demanded. The alarm of fire given by the Congregational bell or later by the town bell brought the firemen running to the engine house where they would grab the engine and run to the fire. If a team of horses happened to be handy, they would be pressed into service. More ingenious was the idea of hitching the engine to the back of a passing trolley car and bumping off up the tracks to the fire. (We had trolleys here from 1895 to 1920.) The spirit of the firemen has been beautifully preserved for posterity in the lines of a lovely sonnet composed in March 1904 by Mr. Elias Andrews (of South Essex). The occasion was the burning of South Essex' Harlow Hotel. It went like this:

Early last month at 12 in the night
The South Essex people awoke with a fright
They heard the alarm of the deep-sounding bell
That told of a fire at the Harlow Hotel.

The fire raged fierce—it grew hotter and hotter.
While we had plenty of sundries we were damned short of water.
Why it's been so dry in South Essex of late,
We've had to take our sundries straight!

They placed No. 2 at Dr. Hull's well
And she wouldn't raise water if they went to—Well
Some raved and some swore South Essex was a goner
Because of no water on Burnham's corner.

Do or say what we would we could get no stream on
Till they came over from Essex with the old Amazon.
In all fights like that with the demon of flame,
You will find that the Amazon always is game.
South Essex was saved, though the hotel is gone;
Thank God for the men of the old Amazon.

Abram Perkins was a man of strong and determined character as was so often the case among folks of rural localities, such as Essex, in the years gone by. Furthermore he didn't hold much with going to church. However, one of the relatives died and he more or less felt compelled, as a token of respect, to go to the funeral, so he dressed up in his best suit and set off at the appointed time for the Congregational Church. He was not, however, without the company of his constant friend and companion, his big black dog. Upon arrival, the pair of them went in and proceeded to a seat only to be met with horrified remonstrances from others of the family already arrived.

"If this place ain't good enough for the dog, it ain't good enough for me neither!" said Abram, "so I guess we'll both go home."

Again more remonstrances and pleading until at length Abram stayed and sat in a pew with the dog sitting up beside him.

This story was told to me by my good friend Mr. Palmer S. Perkins, the assistant postmaster of Essex and a great grandson of Abram. Palmer himself was a purposeful character and inclined to look at things from the practical point of view.

He opened up the post office early one morning and Mr. Alden Burnham came in to get his last night's mail. As he stood at the window Mr. Burnham suddenly slumped to the floor and died. As chance would have it, Harry Cleveland, the town undertaker, happened to come in just then so he and Palmer moved Mr.

Burnham over against the candy counter while Harry went home to get his things and Palmer went out back to look for a cushion. As Palmer said, "Not that it made any difference to Alden whether he had a cushion or not, but it was sort of a matter of sentiment. People coming in would think it odd if he didn't have a cushion or something under his head."

Shortly after a woman came in to buy some stamps. Palmer passed them through the wicket to her just as she looked over and saw Mr. Burnham.

"What's the matter with him?" she asked.

"Nothin' now," said Palmer, "he just died."

Turning pale she backed away from the window in speechless horror and went out without her stamps.

Palmer was the senior deacon at the Congregational Church for some years and his duties included standing alongside the minister to assist at ceremonies of baptism. (He was an old bachelor himself.) Many remember the Sunday when, while fond parents stood nervously by, the cover was lifted off the baptismal font to reveal an empty bowl inside. Quick as a flash Palmer sized up the situation and quietly stepped up to the pulpit where he retrieved what was left of the minister's glass of drinking water. Coming back he solemnly poured it into the basin and the ceremony went off without a hitch.

Mr. Leighton Perkins, Palmer's father, operated a general store. This store was exactly the sort of place that one now finds duplicated in museums and which has taken its place in the legend of rural America. As might be expected, the post office was a section of this store. Palmer worked here with his father for a long time. He likes to tell of the little girl whose mother sent her in one day for a large salt fish. He wrapped it up, leaving the tail sticking out for a handle. As it was pouring rain and the gutters were running brooks, he said to her as she went out, "You look out, now, and don't drop him, because if you do he'll go swimming away." In wide-eyed amazement the little girl went out, gingerly clutching the fish by the tail. A day or two later she came back and confronting Palmer she announced, "You know what you told me about that fish?" "Yes," said Palmer. "Well, my mother says it ain't so."

In a back section of the store which looked out over the depot yard was a semi-circle of benches against the walls, in the center of which, standing in a pan of sand, was a large pot-bellied stove. It was here, around this stove, that the men folks would gather to discuss their politics and town affairs. In my mind's eye I can see that place now. Going in as a child to find my father, I would be sort of half afraid of those rows of men dimly curtained beneath the thick blue haze of tobacco smoke and talking of things that meant nothing to me. Someone would always make particular comment about me, which only embarrassed me more and served to make my stay as brief as possible. Sometimes, though, on summer days there would be nobody there, whereupon my friends and I would go and sit there ourselves while we drank a bottle of tonic.

It was here also that local news was passed around, giving rise to much of the earthy humor and stories that still bring a chuckle today. The man who, by common consent of his contemporaries and those who remember him, was undisputed champion of the wits was Charlie Sam, or more properly, Charles H. Story. Said Charlie, "If you want to make a million dollars, it's easy. All you got to do is to raise a million hens and sell 'em for a dollar apiece." Concerning Essex weather he said, "What we have around here is 9 months of winter and 3 months of damn cold weather."

"I never take a drink of water," said Charlie, "except on the day after the Fourth of July. That's to put out the fire." One day as Leonard Austin (Story) plodded by the post office behind his skinny old horse, Charlie called out, "Leonard, I think I can tell what you feed that horse."

"What?" said Leonard.

"Barrels," said Charlie, "because I can see the staves sticking out."

Perhaps no man ever hit the nail on the head more squarely than Charlie Sam when he made his classic observations: "If you want the winter to go quick, all you need to do is arrange to have a note come due in the spring. Before you know it, the winter's gone."

His best one concerned the seed salesman or drummer as they used to be called. He was seated in Richardson's store behind the stove one day when the drummer came in and after selling Mr. Richardson a stock of seeds for the spring trade prevailed upon Charlie Sam to try some of his cucumber seeds.

A couple of months later he was back and there was Charlie again behind the stove. "Tell me, Mr. Story, did you try my cucumber seeds?" asked the drummer. "I certainly did," replied Charlie.

"How did they grow?"

"Grow!" said Charlie. "Let me tell you how they grew. I planted them just the way you said to do and then as it was sort of warm I went over and sat under a tree for a little rest. I must have dozed off because pretty soon I woke up with an awful chokin' sensation. I put my hand up to my throat and there was a cucumber vine about to strangle me. I reached into my pocket for my jack-knife and pulled out a cucumber big as a squash!"

This store and post office, so completely typical of early rural America, was a gathering place and clearing house for all. Before the days of the railroad or trolley car, it was also a stopping place for the stage lines that ran through town. If a person wanted something out of town and couldn't go after it himself, he wrote on a slate that hung in the post office and the stage driver, reading the message when he arrived, would generally take care of the errand on his next trip.

An experimental telephone was installed here which connected with another phone in Ipswich five miles away. From what I could find out it must have been in the late 1870's, not long after Bell's invention. A large gathering was thrilled at the sound of a bugle coming over the wire clear from the next town.

There were many men who clearly loved to hold forth to the gang around the stove. One of these who especially liked to tell of his exploits in the Civil War and of the jobs he had held was Ike Hewitt. Ike was really carried away one day when one of the boys brought him up short by saying, "Ike, I've been adding up while you talked and if you done all the things you say for as long as you say, it makes you just 172 years old."

Ike was a loyal and devoted member of the Grand Army as was his comrade "Adjutant" Lander who ran a barbershop across the street from the store. Adjutant Lander was Essex's first traffic cop and made an impressive sight in his flowing white whiskers, white gloves and G.A.R. uniform. He was not the only peace officer to make a name for himself, however. Charlie Lane served as constable for many years displaying on at least one occasion the wisdom of Solomon.

He got a complaint one Sunday that a card game was going on upstairs in the firehouse and please, would he investigate. So he did, stomping loudly into the downstairs hall. Going to the foot of the stairs he called out, "You boys ain't playing cards up there, are you?" "Why no, Charlie." "That's what I thought."

It's interesting to note in this era of 9 to 5 or the eight-hour shift that there were those in the old days who believed that life should be more than a daily grind. I had a great-uncle named Abel Story who operated a blacksmith shop on Apple Street by the Essex Falls Brook. The back of his shop hung out over the brook in order to get more floor space inside. Among his town folks Great-uncle Abel had two claims to fame. One was that he never worked in the afternoon and the other was that he once drove in his sleigh from one end of the town to the other and back in the month of May. It seems that a late storm deposited just enough snow to allow him to do it before it all melted.

We have spoken a few pages back about the way the Essex River divided the town into its two major parts. The connecting link between the two was, until 1903, an old wooden drawbridge. The bridge had to be a drawbridge since in those days there were shipyards on the up-river as well as the down-river side. The draw works were hand operated whenever it was necessary to move a new vessel downstream.

As might be imagined, the bridge was a rather crude affair and in its last years became perhaps a little rickety, although it carried the heavy trolley cars over it for many years without incident. However, as was the custom of those days, a circus came marching through town one day on its way to a Gloucester engagement. The procession, or most of it anyway, came down the hill and over the bridge toward South Essex. But then came the elephants. The leading pachyderm placed one foot on the bridge and stopped short. "Nothing doing!" he must have thought to himself. No amount of coaxing could get that elephant to step across the bridge, and if he wouldn't go, the other elephants wouldn't go either. At length the trainers gave up in despair and with assistance from local guides, marched their cautious charges the three miles back through Essex Falls and around Apple Street to South Essex and the Gloucester road.

We had all sorts of interesting people in Essex. Take Gilman Low, for example. Gilman, a south district boy, acquired the reputation of being one of the strongest men of the world not long after the turn of the century. And he did it on a vegetable diet, too. Once, in a prodigious series of exertions, he lifted 1,006,000 lbs. in a span of 34 minutes 35 seconds. On another occasion, with the aid of a specially constructed harness, he raised a load of 2,500 lbs. off the ground, doing it five times in ten seconds.

I have heard it told that Gilman visited the theatre one night in Boston to take in a vaudeville show. Among the acts were a professional strong man and wrestler who took occasion to call for a volunteer from the audience to come up and try a fall or two. Gilman, so the story goes, rose and said he guessed he'd come up and try, whereupon he peeled off his coat, grabbed the performer and tossed him aside like a plucked chicken. The audience was delighted.

Then there was Mildred Abel (Burnham) who in the last years of her life lived alone in a desolate cottage way up on Grove Street. I can see her now as she trudged to the grocery store dressed in a woolen cap, long overcoat and rubber boots and pushing her wheelbarrow. She used to buy cocoa in 10 or 12 lb. lots. Somebody asked her once why she did that and her reply was. "When I want cocoa, I want cocoa!"

A landmark even from far down the Essex River is the steeple of the Congregational Church containing its beloved Paul Revere bell. The church and steeple were erected in 1792 and the bell carries the inscription "REVERE

BOSTON 1797". The note of the bell (high C) is doubly a silver one, since many families of the parish contributed silver spoons and silver dollars to be cast into the bell. For years and years an Essex ship carpenter would begin his day's work, go home to dinner, begin again in the afternoon and quit for the night by the notes of the Revere bell. It gave the alarm of fire, rang out on the glorious Fourth, called the men to town meeting and tolled the death of statesman and humble citizen; all this, of course, in addition to its regular Sunday summons to divine worship. It was also the custom years ago for the sexton to begin as a funeral procession approached the church and toll the bell a number of strokes equal to the age of the deceased.

When I was a boy the sexton was Mr. Ed Lander, a wiry little man who couldn't have weighed much over 100 lbs. How he could handle that 825 lb. bell is a tribute to his perseverance and determination. He could toll the bell all day without once making the clapper bounce, although on several occasions while swinging the bell through its full arc he was carried to the ceiling on the bell rope. Somebody would have to come and pull him down. I remember in the winter that he would stick his head through the rear door of the auditorium about 20 minutes before service time and blow loudly through puckered lips. If he couldn't see his breath the place was warm enough.

The present building is actually the fourth one to be used by this congregation. How they raised the first one is quite an interesting story in itself.

As mentioned before, the town of Essex had originally been known as Chebacco Parish in the town of Ipswich. It was first settled in 1634 and was (and is) about five miles from the center of Ipswich. It had been the custom of those then living here to repair to this center of the town on each Sunday of the year to attend services of Divine worship. This hazardous and trying journey on foot each week did not seem too burdensome at first, so glad were the settlers to be enjoying their hard-won religious freedom. However, with the advent of a new generation, this circumstance became somewhat vexing to the end that the residents here petitioned the great and general court for leave to build a church edifice and call a pastor of their own.

Probably the prospect of the mother church's losing a large segment of its membership along with their valuable financial support inspired in the leadership of that church a strong determination to prevent that from happening, and the result was a protracted legal struggle to do so. In the chance that they might eventually win out, the men of Chebacco proceeded in high spirits to select a site and frame out the structure of a fine church building. This framework was all made and carefully laid out on the ground ready to be raised when news suddenly came that the people of Ipswich, who had greater influence in the colonial legislature than Chebacco people did, had finally succeeded in having an order issued enjoining the men of Chebacco from erecting their own church.

These tidings were received with great sorrow and disappointment in the parish, but not however to one of the good women, Mrs. Abigail Varney, who detected in the order what she felt to be the key to the whole situation. Accordingly, she gathered some of her friends to a tea party one spring afternoon in 1679. As they talked about the dismal turn of events she pointed out to them that the order prevented the men from raising the church. It didn't say anything about the women doing it. An exclamation of delighted approval greeted her reasoning, and the next day saw the women riding off in several directions to the neighboring villages of Manchester and Gloucester from which they returned bringing with them a large band of men from those towns who had volunteered to come and raise the new church.

They turned to with a will and, while Chebacco men stood by without laying a hand to the proceedings, the new edifice soon stood proudly in its appointed place. A fine feast and celebration climaxed the endeavors and Chebacco, finally, had its church. As a kind of sour-grapes gesture the Ipswich authorities had the women arrested but nothing really could be done and after ordering the women to apologize to the court, the proceedings were dropped. Having demonstrated themselves to be a people possessed of far more than the ordinary degree of zeal and determination, it was quite appropriate that these men and women of Chebacco should choose for their leader a man of far more than the ordinary degree of conviction, enthusiasm and ability. A young graduate of Harvard College, their man was compounded of equal parts of patriot, libertarian, businessman and divine. His name was John Wise.

In a pastorate here which was destined to extend for 45 years from 1680 until his death in 1725, John Wise not only was a spiritual bulwark for his flock, but plunged with an eager heart into the burgeoning spirit of rebellion against the growing oppression of English rule. He also took a vigorous part in the cause of democracy and autonomy among the Congregational churches and championed the cause of inoculation for smallpox when such a stand was highly unpopular. He served as a military chaplain in the expedition against French Canada; he took a lively interest in civic affairs of his community; he farmed the 65 acres given him by the parish with competence; he carried on several successful commercial ventures and all this while raising a fine family of five sons and two daughters. The house he built for himself in 1703 is today one of Essex's treasured landmarks.

A list of accomplishments such as this would, of itself, mark John Wise as an outstanding man, but more than these, the people of our town have ever been proud of the fact that history shows him to have been the man who, perhaps more than any other, was responsible for igniting the spark which ultimately was fanned into the conflagration of the American Revolution. He it was who first gave utterance to the principle that "taxation without representation is tyranny!" This expression of feeling, voiced in August 1687, came on the occasion of his protestations against the tax imposed on the colonists by the British governor Sir Edmond Andros. As a result John Wise and several other Ipswich men were put in jail. The immediate issue was soon resolved, but the spark had been ignited. Every school child has learned from the history books what happened in our country from that point on.

For the first two hundred years of its history, the parish of Chebacco, later to become the town of Essex, was strictly a Congregational community. If one went to church at all, he went to the Congregational Church. If one wished to vote, he must first join the Congregational Church. As in all the colonies during this period religion and matters of doctrine here were very seriously considered. On several occasions in parish history splinter groups separated themselves from the main church body, although remaining fundamentally Congregationalist.

However, in 1836, a group left the faith to form one of the new Universalist societies. This act, as might be imagined, created quite a cleavage among the inhabitants of the town. Those who went to one church would emphatically have no part of the other. Feelings were especially keen when members of the same household or family took opposite stands. Mr. Nehemiah Burnham and his wife would walk down from Essex Falls Sunday after Sunday, parting company at the square, she to walk up the hill to the Congregational Church, and he to step over to the Universalist. Then there were two brothers, one a Universalist, the other a Congregationalist. The Universalist brother died first and the story goes that it took the other a long time to make up his mind to go to his brother's funeral. Though not in the ways it did years ago, religion has played a prominent role in the lives and affairs of the town right down to the present day.

In 1911 a wave of excitement ran through the town as the power company ran its lines along the streets in preparation for the installation of electric lights. Mr. Kavanagh, the druggist in South Essex, decided it would be nice to have a ceremonial lighting up of his store when the power was turned on and so proceeded with enthusiasm to get his wires up and fixtures installed.

Across the street was the general store of Mr. C. C. Burnham who noted Mr. Kavanagh's plans with some interest. Here was a chance for some fun, thought Mr. Burnham. The working crews of the light company were on the friendliest terms with him, so that a few whispered suggestions and other miscellaneous inducements were enough to turn the trick.

The night of the great turning on finally came and quite a crowd gathered in the street in front of Kavanagh's drug store, presumably in response to his publicity. At the appointed hour, as the group waited in hushed expectancy, the power came and C.C. Burnham's store shone out in a blaze of electric illumination while poor Kavanagh's remained unaccountably dark.

It's curious how an event, deadly serious at the time of its occurrence becomes somewhat comical with the passage of time. There's nothing funny about a house catching fire, but what people do at such a time is often funny when thought about afterward, as for example when Charlie Henry Story's house caught fire. The family threw two mirrors out of the upstairs window, after which they proceeded to lug mattresses down the stairs. Annie Tarr ran out of her smoking house carrying a dish of cold boiled potatoes.

In a somewhat different vein, it will be remembered that years ago a milkman would deliver the milk into the family's own containers. Marshall Cogswell, in delivering the milk one morning for his father, knocked at a door and called out for something to put the milk in. A few moments passed with no reply, whereupon the door opened a little and an arm holding an empty chamber pot was thrust out at him.

Then let us consider the case of poor Wallingford Todd Burnham. His mother had said that she would name her son so that he couldn't be nicknamed. Wallingford set out his first day of school and the other children, seeing his approach down the road, called out, "Here comes that Wallopin' Toad", and Wallopin' Toad he remained the rest of his life.

Speaking of nicknames, and for those who are interested, there were quite a few among Essex residents worthy of note. Try these: Billy Tunk, Billy Wap, Johnny Quick-step, Emily Pop, Susie Mink, or Shinny Billy. Or these: Beefy, Squawk, Tonk, Clip, Toofy, Needles or Custard. Some were more descriptive: No-nosed Epes, Sore-Eyed Isaac, Lily Hump, Chocolate or The Dummy. That's enough to demonstrate that in Essex they called a spade a spade.

If one lived in a small town such as Essex in those by-gone years it wasn't necessary to accomplish an earth-shaking feat to gain recognition among one's fellows. Just so simple an occurrence as coming home a little late and maybe a little tipsy could turn the trick. Amri (long I) Story's return one night gained him a fame that carried over for years. Banging loudly on his door in a fashion to wake the whole neighborhood he shouted for his wife to come down and let him in. Just to make sure it was the right man, she herself called out, "Is that you, Amri?"

"Am I Amri? If I ain't Amri, who in hell am I?" was the answer. That did it. No man ever mentioned the name of Amri again without adding, "If I ain't Amri, who in hell am I?"

Robert Burnham, who lived with his sister Amanda, thought he would try and raise his own tobacco one year. He was honored for his pains in a verse of a typical song of the minstrels the following year, which went:

> *Tobacco is a filthy weed*
> *And Robert Burnham sows the seed.*
> *It stains his pockets, scents his clothes,*
> *Makes Mandy Bob turn up her nose!*

A curious aberration of the human make-up is that which produces a miser. There have always been misers and no doubt always will be, but somehow they seemed to achieve more prominence years ago than they do now. I think they took more unabashed relish in the practice of miserliness than we do. People didn't worry in the old days about whether or not they seemed queer to their fellows. They were more inclined to do as they pleased.

As might be expected, we had some misers in Essex. The reader, I hope, will understand that as one who must continue to live in a small town with the relatives of these people, the writer is reluctant to be too specific about names in a matter of this kind. Suffice it to say that there were Burnhams, Storys, Andrewses and others. Perhaps an example or two would show the extent to which an Essex miser could go.

Essex farmers would sell their milk to regional distributors or wholesalers who, of course, supplied the large metal cans in which the milk was collected. We had one old farmer who would take new cans and proceed to bang them with a rock or a hammer. The dents thus produced would reduce the actual capacity of a can a little bit, although he, of course, was paid for its stated contents.

There was an old ship carpenter who made it his practice to hire a rig once a year and drive himself and his family to Salem to purchase clothes and household effects for the ensuing year. He once arrived at the bridge connecting the cities of Beverly and Salem to find that a toll of two cents was required to pass over. He put up a loud and lengthy argument but to no avail. The toll-taker was adamant and collected his two cents. However, our friend was determined to triumph and when he returned to Essex he came by a much longer and more circuitous route.

Another man of this same family courted a girl from Topsfield. It was his custom to walk the intervening ten miles with his shoes in his hand. He would stop and put them on as he approached her house. He prided himself all his life on the fact that he never burned any coal. All his fuel was shipyard wood he would bring home under his arm.

In an earlier section I mentioned the sawing of the planks with the so-called pit saw. A young man one brutally hot summer day was engaging himself with the lower end of one of these saws. The old bulldog of a ship carpenter on the upper end was abusing the boy to the point where he began to cough and spit blood. At this point the boy's father, one of the town's noted misers, who also worked in the yard, came by and seeing the lad's distress called to the foreman, "We can't have him down there," he said. "Find something else for him to do!" Mind you, he didn't suggest that the boy go home to rest and recuperate. That would have meant loss of part of the day's wage.

In this same vein was a shipyard man who, late in the week, was struck in the eye by a piece of flying metal. He took himself to the doctor who caused him to be hospitalized for the removal of the eye. He was out of work for several months, during which time he paid all his own expenses and medical bills. When at length he returned to work he reminded the yard owner that he still had $11.50 coming to him as wages for the week in which he had been hurt. "Why so you have," said the owner, and passed him $12.00.

"I don't happen to have 50 cents in change," said our friend.

"Oh, that's all right," replied the yard owner magnanimously. "You can let it go!"

Two acquaintances of mine worked one summer for a farmer who, with his family, had one of the finest reputations for miserliness Essex ever had. They worked long and hard one day getting in salt hay. In order to get the last load into the barn before dark they went without supper and finally, with the hay safely stowed and darkness upon them, their employer disappeared into the house to get something to eat. In a few minutes he reappeared with a little box and with great solemnity presented each with one soda cracker. As he munched on his own he observed: "There's lots of virtue in a cracker!" As a final gesture he took the empty cracker box and carefully folding it up stowed it under the seat of the wagon.

"What are you doing that for?" asked my friends.

"Why, the ashes are worth something!"

From time immemorial every small country town has had its characters, those solitary individuals who, for one reason or another, strike out against the tide of popular thought or behavior.

Essex has always had an abundance of interesting characters. Many have already been mentioned, but there were still others. Men like Gilbert Orne (Burnham) who often chopped away a hole in the river ice so that he could take his regular winter day's dip, or Albert Cogswell who liked to scratch in the frost on the barn window the reassuring legend "I'm worth $90,000." None of them, however, could hold a candle to America Burnham or simply Meriky, as he was known to all.

If America Burnham were living today, he would probably be confined to an institution. Even for his own time he was startling in many ways. He prophesized the future, he talked about God, he went into the woods to live off the land and sometimes went about with a rubber boot on one foot and an overshoe on the other. This, he said, made him prepared for any kind of weather.

"Meriky" called himself a prophet of God and the printed religious handbills he passed out were signed, "America Burnham—Prophet." They also carried this footnote:

"This message of prophecy has been overlooked (meaning looked over) by the Spirit of God, and stood 40 days for examination after it was first wrote; and then accepted to be correct as ordered; and if any person copies it off they must be careful not to change a word of it."

He had an awesome respect for what he considered to be God's laws and did his best to abide by them. If man-made laws or regulations conflicted in any way with his interpretation of God's laws he simply ignored them. His principal occupation was digging clams and not infrequently he found himself in Court charged with improperly digging on the flats of adjoining towns. His defense was simple. They were God's clams in God's earth and were there for anyone to take. Moreover, he saw no need to respect an earthly courtroom or an earthly judge and adopted an attitude of total in difference to whatever happened in the courtroom. It got so that he gathered an enthusiastic following, some one of which usually paid his fines. The judges learned to make allowances for him and America simply went his way. He even defied the U. S. Customs Department when he put out in his little fishing vessel. All vessels are supposed to be registered and have a name and port from which they hail. America's was called *Angel Gabriel* and hailed from The Kingdom of Heaven. He steadfastly refused to change it and apparently the regional custom house gave it all up as a bad job. I've heard it said that *Angel Gabriel* was the only unregistered vessel to sail out of Gloucester.

America had an interesting origin. He was born about 1820 in the cabin of a fishing vessel lying in Frenchman's Cove, Maine. His father, captain of the vessel, was a Burnham and his mother was a Low. They were unmarried. Presumably they came from Essex because they returned not long afterward and America spent most of his life here. He had a half-sister, his mother's child by another man, with whom he lived for a great many years. She had married a sea-faring man named Prindle who brought her clothes and finery from all over the world. When she was left a widow it is thought she came home to keep house for America. Everyone knew her as Miz Prindle. She was a faithful member of the Congregational Church to which she repaired on Sunday mornings decked out in a brilliant green dress, a monstrous hat with wild flowers on it (underneath she wore 20-penny spikes for hairpins) and finally a large bustle. It was always her custom when thus attired to parade down the middle of the road and upon reaching the meeting house to walk to the front of the sanctuary, turn around and pick out a suitable seat. When she took sick she would dress up and walk the mile or more to Doctor Town's office. After telling him of her trouble she would summon him to pay her a visit after which she would walk home again and climb into bed to await the doctor's arrival.

As has been mentioned Meriky was a clammer. However, he also spent much time fishing, lobstering, eeling and, in the summer, berry-picking. He had a good natural ability in the use of tools and developed a great proficiency as a boat-builder. He constructed several fine boats for himself, all of which were excellent sailors. One of these he called the *Dahlia*. He incorporated features of design which were considered radical at the time, but which proved themselves in use. He constructed one boat wholly without the use of money, making everything himself. When he got to the sails and rigging he was finally persuaded to accept a loan, although assuring the lender that he "calculated to pay" if his fishing should prosper. This boat, his *Angel Gabriel*, was a fairly good sized, pinky-styled schooner. Mr. Ed Perkins of whom we have spoken, told me he remembered well the occasion of her launching.

Meriky pursued other mechanical projects, inventing a device that he called the teltone, a scheme for communication through the air. Although turning down his application for a patent the U. S. Patent Office encouraged him to continue his research. He prophesied the coming of the airplane when, as he said, "People will fly like birds." In this connection he made a parachute-like device and proceeded to fly off a roof. It must have worked to some extent because the leap didn't kill him.

He was very wise in the ways of nature. He understood the signs of the weather, the lore of the woods and he discovered the health-giving properties of many plants and herbs and especially of blueberries and punkin-seed oil. He worked out methods of subsistence for a person in the wilds. He disappeared once into the woods and after 40 days a crowd went looking for him. They finally found him, but he refused to be rescued.

To earn a living it was his custom to go about the streets from house to house peddling his clams. He carried them in a large bucket, ladling them out with great precision. For a time he conceived the idea that the use of money was sinful and steadfastly refused to allow his customers to pay for their clams. Miz Prindle was more of a practical turn of mind, however, and when her brother got notions like this, she took it upon herself to follow discreetly behind and make the collections herself after America had passed on to the next house.

The urge to preach and to prophesy was very strong in America Burnham. Usually it was his custom to hold his own outdoor services. A favorite pulpit was the outside stairway to the garret of a small shop that stood in front of the Story shipyard. However, if necessary, a pile of timber did just as well. Printed handbills would announce the time, place and subject. It made no difference to America whether anyone showed up or not. Even if nobody came he preached just the same. One of his sermons was delivered to a single, small and overawed boy. However, he sometimes felt compelled to carry his message to church. Perhaps the idea of a captive audience attracted him. He would not sit long in a pew but would get up and stride to the pulpit. On several occasions the minister was forced to come down and almost wrestle in the aisle with him to keep him out of the pulpit. It got so they had to keep a lookout to warn of America's approach and waylay him before he could get inside.

Believe it or not, he managed a stunt like this in the chamber of the House of Representatives in Washington, D.C. In the belief that Congress and the Government should be reorganized along lines of greater brotherly love, he traveled with an Essex man, Capt. Butler, in his ship to Baltimore. Then setting out on foot he walked to Washington and made his way into the Capitol building. Having watched for an opportunity, he seized upon a relatively unguarded moment of informality among the representatives and before anyone knew what was up a voice rang out from the speaker's rostrum: "Thus saith the Lord--." He never got any further. A thunderstruck House made a dive for this apparition and poor America was hustled for the nearest exit. I presume he was arrested and held for trial, but the representative for our district, a man who had spent much time in Essex, recognized old America and interceded in his behalf, sending him back to Miz Prindle without further incident. She, at least, didn't put up with his nonsense. If he got too cantankerous where she was concerned she simply took the broom to him and drove him out of the house along with the chickens.

In his declining years after the death of Miz Prindle, America lived alone in a little shack near the riverbank down on Clay Point. In spite of his fierce independence the Overseer of the Poor finally persuaded him to pay a visit, as they said, to the Town Farm. At first he wouldn't stay, but each time he left he would come back and stay a little longer, until finally he became a permanent resident, remaining there to the end.

A more fitting tribute and memorial to America Burnham could not be found—one of the finest and most productive clam flats in the Town of Essex was named, and is called to this day, America's Bank.

The presence of the shipyards in Essex gave rise to numerous supporting industries or trades and a walk about the town in the latter years of the nineteenth century would reveal many interesting activities going on in the back yards and shops all over town.

On Pickering Street, a stone's throw from the post office was the last and largest ropewalk where cotton lines of various sizes, both plain and tarred, were made for use as trawls aboard the fishing schooners. This was known as the Mears Improved Line Co. and was operated by Mr. Henry William Mears. (His father who operated it before him was William Henry.) The principal building was a long narrow shed-like structure that stretched along behind the houses for nearly 450 feet. The curious rope making machinery was steam operated. I have a piece of beautiful cotton rope made there which is still as strong and supple as when it was spun probably 50 years ago.

At Essex Falls, in a shop behind the house on Martin Street where his grandson now lives, was the place where Bert Noah (Story) and later his sons Harry and Leonard made the great wooden anchor windlasses for the vessels. This shop, by the way, was still operated as late as 1930. Theirs was a brisk business since nearly every vessel needed an anchor windlass. Some of these were tremendously heavy affairs and all took many hours of careful work to round out the drums and fit the several iron parts, ratchets, bands, etc. which were part of the device.

Both Leonard and Harry Story were old bachelors, and Leonard, or Len, as he was more commonly known, had the interesting habit of eating some of his meals in the cellar down by the furnace. It was also his custom never to remove his hat indoors or out. Harry was more of a lady's man and I can remember him, when well past seventy, he poked along across the causeway to South Essex at about 9 in the evening with an umbrella under his arm and carrying a pint of ice cream over to a lady friend. Harry had been an artist in his younger days, displaying considerable talent with the brush. He turned out many beautiful landscapes and several types of floral decorations. Curiously, he gave it all up and turned to ship work.

One of the greatest artisans the town of Essex ever knew lived two houses beyond Bert Noah. This was George Claiborne, a man in whose hands the use of tools became a talent of the highest order. He was principally a stone mason yet he seemed to be able to create other things with equal ease. A monument to George Claiborne's skill stands today in the wall surrounding what was once

Harry Story (left) and Arthur Gates about 1930. The scene is the spar yard of Charles H. Andrews. They are working on the 90-foot mainmast of the yacht *Constellation*.

an estate of the late renowned Henry Clay Frick in Hamilton, Mass. A more beautifully executed piece of stonework, part of it laid up without the use of mortar, is seldom seen anywhere.

George Claiborne was particularly remembered about Essex, however, for the wonderful wooden pumps he made for the vessels. He also built several boats in his shop at Essex Falls. He could get quite upset at times. There were those who recalled the beautiful motorboat he built for a client of considerable wealth and influence. A disagreement developed at the completion of the job, however, and for some reason the owner refused to make his final payment, whereupon George, in a fit of pique, seized his broadaxe and stove in the garboard planks.

In the course of his various contracting jobs, Mr. Claiborne had frequent occasion to use dynamite. As a matter of fact, he became quite captivated with the thrill and noise of the explosions and enthusiastically carried on private celebrations of the Fourth of July. There used to be a little building in Coffill's Hollow near the town hall where some of the boys gathered to play cards. As sort of a joke, George put a large dynamite charge out behind it one Saturday night and let 'er go. You should have seen the fellows come out of there. The first one to emerge came through the screen door without bothering to open it. His celebrations of the Fourth were carried out with a brass yacht-club cannon. One year a miscellaneous charge of rocks, sticks and whatnot went right through the front of the Essex Falls grammar school located across the street.

The many sides of his nature were perhaps most beautifully illustrated in the lovely poems he composed. He would never write them down but carried in his head verse upon verse of stories and recollections of his boyhood, friends and scenes about the town. Fortunately, his wife prevailed upon him to recite several of them in order that she might write them down before he died.

To return to our story, there were shops of several other kinds in addition to these we have mentioned. There must have been a half dozen blacksmith shops where ironwork for the ships was made. This ironwork was principally composed of the many eyes and bands for the masts and spars and the chain plates for the sides of the hull to which the rigging was attached. The tackle blocks of the rigging, in turn, were also made in the local block-shops, one of which stood on what is now my next-door neighbor's lawn.

The making by hand of a great wooden mast is a craft that must take its place along with so many others in the pages of history. We had one of the country's last wooden spar yards in Essex, operated earlier by Mr. Timothy Andrews and lastly by his son Charles Hanson Andrews. Charlie Hanson was known for miles around and had friends wherever he went. He not only made masts for the vessels but also large wooden derricks used in various construction industries. Then, too, his flagstaffs could be found in almost any town of the county.

The logs from which any type of wooden spar is made are always referred to as sticks. The sticks used by Mr. Andrews were sometimes nearly 80 or 90 feet long and came in by railroad using up the length of two or three flat cars. In making the spars it was the custom to place them on a series of low wooden trestles and after peeling off the bark, they would be hewed to a square section. The square section was then made octagonal after which, with draw knives and planes, they were made smooth and round. The skill came, not only in the use of the broadaxe and drawknife, but in the ability to lay out the tapering lines by which the stick was cut. The lines of taper often had to be adjusted to compensate for variances of grain or disposition of knots or even some times to dodge a scar left in the tree by a bolt of lightning. Furthermore, even though most trees have a sweep or crook in the trunk, the centerline of a completed mast had to be perfectly straight. Charlie Hanson was a master at all this. "And you know," he told me once, "you have to have a round eye to make a spar." What he meant was that it was necessary to tell just by looking whether a finished mast was perfectly round.

Rough sticks were stored pending use in two or three little tidal creeks adjoining the spar yard. Here they were preserved by the salt water and also made a beautiful place for kids to play. As a boy I spent hours down around the spar yard leaping about on the floating logs racing from end to end of the great sticks. Another thing that was fun was to put an ear against one end of a long stick as it lay there on its trestles. Someone else would then go to the other end of the log and scratch on it ever so lightly with a nail or finger. No matter how gently it was touched the noise was perfectly transmitted along the length of the log to the listener at the other end.

Many of Mr. Andrews' spars were made for my father, Arthur D. Story. Father had lent him some money at one time with which to buy some sticks, taking a note for the sum involved. For some reason Mr. Andrews could not meet the note when it came due and a while after, Father met Charles on the street and said:

"Charles, what about that note? I'm getting worried about it."

"Why Arthur, are you worrying about that, too?"

"Yes, Charles, I am."

"Well then," said Charles, "I'll stop worrying. There's no need of two of us worrying about it!"

For a time Mr. Andrews had charge of my class of boys in the Congregational Sunday School. I don't remember that he taught us a great deal about the Bible, but week after week we sat enchanted while he regaled us with stories of his many adventures, his spars and where they went, and of the many interesting people he encountered in his travels. (Some yardarms he made for the Bear of Oakland went to Antarctica with Admiral Byrd on his first expedition.) He had a beautiful baritone voice, too, and joyfully led us all in many stirring renditions of the old gospel hymns. I will never hear the strains of The Old Rugged Cross without fondly recalling Charles Hanson Andrews as he sang it for us in the old Sunday School.

In speaking of the local enterprises supported by the shipyards, I must mention the teamsters. Beginning in 1874, when the local branch of the Eastern Railroad was put into operation, the great proportion of the lumber used in the yards was brought into Essex on the railroad. The depot and freight yards were located in the center of town and it was the job of the teamsters to move it from the depot to the shipyard. They were possessed of magnificent spans of horses and rugged high-wheeled wagons that they drew up right alongside the loaded freight cars. The timbers were then rolled off onto the wagons.

Vessel planking, for the most part, consisted of long oak planks, two and three inches or more thick. Some of this stuff was nearly 70 feet long, requiring two flat cars to hold it. When loaded on the wagons, it hung way out over the horses' heads in front and sometimes dragged on the ground behind. It made an impressive sight as it moved through the streets to the shouts of the drivers.

In A.D. Story's yard the timber storage area was the slope of a fairly steep hill at the rear of the yard. It took a high degree of skill to handle the big and heavy wagons down the grade and around the sharp turn into the yard. On more than one occasion I have heard it said, the brakes on the wagon have let go and allowed the entire load to come against the horses. Noble and intelligent beasts that they were, rather than run away down the hill and into the creek, they would instinctively hold the load back and of their own accord turn into the yard at the proper place.

I hold in my wallet a little card that signifies that I have been appointed by the select of Essex to be an official Surveyor of wood and bark. This office has come to be merely a traditional one now, a sort of sentimental holdover from the old days when the surveyor of lumber and the surveyor of wood and bark had a real job to do. No one knows how many millions of feet of timber have come into Essex for use in the shipyards, but it was this man's job to measure it, or scale it, if you will, and certify that the buyer was getting what he was billed for. Mr.

Frank McKenzie held this job for many years and it was he who worked along with the teamsters measuring the pieces as they rolled off onto the wagons. It was also his job, if requested, to go into the woods and estimate the amount of timber standing in a lot, or scale the footage in a pile of logs.

No account of the businesses and industries of Essex would be complete without some mention of the ice business. It was, of course, in no way concerned with the shipbuilding industry, nor was it in any sense unique in our town, but its presence contributed much to the general economic prosperity, of the town and provided much tonnage for our local branch of the Eastern, later the Boston and Maine railroad. The various aspects of and circumstances peculiar to the ice business have been more or less thoroughly dealt with by several authors, so there is no need to treat of them again here. However, I must mention one thing that still evokes an outburst of heated reminiscence from anyone who re members the events—the ice house fires.

We had some monumental icehouses on the shores of our Chebacco Lake and they burned down on several occasions with resulting monumental conflagrations. I remember two of these occasions myself. On one the fire started somewhere around the machinery that operated the conveyors and on the other, the houses were struck by lightning.

The greatest and worst of these fires occurred on March 25, 1910. The weather on that day was extraordinary for so early in the year, being about 90 degrees, with a strong westerly gale. It was claimed that the fire started from a railroad section crew's bonfire near the tracks. In any case, before anything much could be done the biggest house, belonging to Mr. Charles Mears, was a mass of flame with a deluge of sparks and embers falling into the dry woods and fields and onto houses a mile away. Before long some neighboring icehouses belonging to Mr. Enoch Story were also in flames and nearly half the town rushed to do battle. Lacking anything but a couple of hand-tubs there was little the firefighters could do other than to try to stop the fires in the woods and fields and keep them from coming around the houses of Essex Falls.

As chance would have it a great fire was also in progress in the neighboring town of Hamilton. Here no less than 22 dwellings were to be consumed, causing help in the form of a large steam pumper to be sent by railroad from the City of Salem. Since the pumper sat on a railroad car it was found impossible to use it to advantage or to get it near enough to a body of water from which it could draft, so an engine was coupled on again and the pumper with its crew sent down the Essex Branch to help put out at the ice house fires. Sadly, however, all this effort proved futile, since by the time the pumper arrived the ice houses were flat and furthermore, the crew that came with it was so far under the weather they didn't know whether they were in Essex or New York City.

The lower reaches of the Essex River, together with those of other similar tidal inlets which find their way up among the marshes of our town form a lovely landlocked little bay having beautiful islands and picturesque patches of sand and marsh grasses and enclosed by miles of magnificent beaches and dunes. In the years particularly since World War II this region has been discovered by thousands of vacationers to be a veritable paradise of hitherto unspoiled sea, marsh, sand and sky. As the hosts of happy fun-seekers split the waves with their powerboats and water skis there is nothing to indicate to them that this very area, besides containing the best clam flats in the world, was once a part of the commerce of the region in that it was the loading place for the sanders. They were the little old sailing ships that had been relegated to the business of carrying beach sand to the foundries and manufacturing concerns of Boston and nearby cities. Many were the ships that put in at Essex Bay for sand. After anchoring and securing the ship, long wooden ramps were put ashore and the sand was brought out by men and wheelbarrows. It would take two or three days to load, then off they went.

In the warrant for the annual Town Meeting for this year will be an article that will read, "To see what action the Town wishes to take in regard to its clam industry and raise, assess and appropriate money for the same." This article was there last year, the year before that, and for almost as many years as we've been having town meetings. In other words, the clam industry of the town of Essex began when the first settlers arrived in 1634 or 1635 and has continued without interruption down to the present day.

Few people enjoy the freedom of thought and action that a clammer does. He has but one real boss and that is the tide. Except as his digging is regulated by the going and coming of the tide he can do and say just about what he wants—and usually does. Clamming is, perforce, a rugged life, albeit a healthy one. It used to take real stamina to row down the river every day, summer and winter, and bring back a barrel of clams dug one at a time. The clammers use outboard motors now, but they still have to dig the clams in the same old way. Fortunately they still taste the same old way.

Clamming and shipbuilding have made Essex famous for centuries, but now with shipbuilding gone, we must look to the clams to maintain a name for Essex. The clam industry perhaps means more to Essex now than ever, for with modern modes and habits of travel it carries the name of Essex to all parts of the globe.

An offshoot of the clam industry in Essex has been the establishment here of several fine summer restaurants which specialize in clams, lobsters and seafoods.

The biggest sailing ship ever built in Essex was the *Mattie Atwood* of 653 gross tons in 1872.

One of the earliest of these was Callahan's Riverside House, established by Mr. Leonard Callahan about 1922. The fame and reputation of these restaurants, and particularly Callahan's, spread to the point where a friend of mine, himself a loyal patron, sat at lunch one day in a restaurant in Grand Central Terminal, New York City. He was suffering through a bowl of New York clam chowder when he overheard the man next to him, also having clam chowder, say to his companion. "Golly, this stuff doesn't taste much like the clam chowder we get up at Callahan's!"

Who can say how many bushels of clams have come from the tidal flats of the Essex River? In three hundred years of digging it must run into millions. We have always said that as long as we had our clams no one here need starve, no matter how tough the times.

So it is seen that the life of Essex has been inexorably molded by its little tidal river; the farmers who gathered salt hay from the hundreds of acres of marshland, the clammers who waited for the ebbing tide to uncover the flats, and the shipbuilder who launched his vessels upon the flowing waters. The feelings of an Essex man for his home, family and river are beautifully summed up by the one who uttered the immortal words—"There are two things in this world I wouldn't lend. One is my wife and the other is my eel spear."

five

Launchings

IMAGINE, IF YOU WILL, A bright and beautiful spring day. A gentle westerly breeze ruffles the surface of the Essex River as it rises with the incoming tide. Down in one of the shipyards a sleek new schooner stands on the ways ready to take her maiden dip, black hull glistening in the sunshine, streams of pennants fluttering from thin poles. Let us imagine further that this is one of the famous fishermen's cup defenders (racers, we called them), perhaps the *Mayflower*, *Puritan*, *Columbia*, or the great *Gertrude L. Thebaud*. The newspapers have been writing for some time about the vessel and word of her completion has gathered a great crowd along the causeway in the center of town to see her launch.

The streets are lined with cars, some from distant places, and soon every vantage point is black with eager spectators. A curious hush of interest and expectancy pervades the atmosphere. People seem to speak almost in whispers. Suddenly a cry "Here comes the tugboat," and as the great tug steams slowly into view around the bend we hear the sound of hammers and mauls begin to ring out from around the schooner. The men are knocking out the keel blocks and wedging up the vessel onto her cradle. Their progress can be dimly followed through the structure of the launching ways and the tension and excitement increase by the minute as they work their way forward. Here and there a scholarly spectator points out to his neighbors the details of what is taking place. At length the men emerge from behind the cribbing and the last exciting phase is about to begin. The moment of launching is at hand.

When the *Gertrude L. Thebaud* was launched in 1930, the Essex schools were closed so that the children might watch the event.

First a brief pause ensues while the sponsor mounts a little stand clutching in her trembling hands the brightly beribboned bottle of fine champagne. Then two pairs of stalwart ship carpenters take their places at the upper ends of the two sliding ways, each pair taking up a freshly sharpened cross-cut saw. Now at a word from the foreman two great saws begin to move in unison with the command, "Stop at your first mark." As the first mark, indicating depth of cut on the ways is reached, comes another pause and again a command: "Take your second mark!" Again the saws move as one, only to stop as the next mark, an inch deeper, is reached. The tension becomes almost unbearable. A mere one inch of thickness is all that remains to hold the vessel.

But this is the moment. The foreman, clenching his fists, shouts to his men "Saw away!" and saw they do, flashing back and forth in their eagerness. Suddenly a loud crack and she's free—she starts. A thousand voices cry, "There she goes!" The sponsor gives a mighty smash with her bottle and amid the tantalizing aroma of the champagne and the smoke of hot grease the towering schooner glides majestically down the ways. Faster she moves until with a graceful plunge and torrential splash she parts the waves for the first time. A welcoming blast from the whistle of the waiting towboat rends the air, a hundred autos take up the chorus and the throng on shore exhales a collective sigh of awe and relief. What a spectacle!

No one who ever saw one of our launchings, particularly as they were carried off in the later years, will ever forget the experience. As the occasions began to be less frequent, the word would spread seemingly everywhere and the people would come from miles around to witness the event. What a contrast to the earlier years. The time was when an Essex vessel came down the ways almost once a week. As a matter of interest the records show that from November 1850 to November 1853 no less than 169 vessels were launched from 15 different shipyards. This is considerably more than one a week. Early photographs in my collection show many vessels being launched with hardy a soul bothering to take notice. People took it for granted, like the air they breathed.

Nevertheless a boat launching has always been an interesting thing and especially the method that Essex builders used to accomplish it. I have alluded in a previous chapter to some launching events and would like to tell more of these noteworthy occasions.

Basically there were two methods used here to slide the boats from shore into the water. The first, which was briefly described in the opening paragraph of this chapter, was the so-called cradle method, used with minor variations for generations in all parts of the world and still used today in most commercial shipyards wherever they may be.

Essentially this is just what the name implies. A cradle (perhaps sled would be a better word) is built under the completed hull and the boat in its cradle slides down a pair of greased tracks or ways into the water in basically the same fashion as a youngster slides down a hill on its sled. Without going into a tedious and wordy description of the details of this process, suffice it to say that while the principle of the thing is of the utmost simplicity, the actual work involved in building a ways and supporting cradle for a heavy ship and then transferring the weight of the ship from the blocking on which she was built to the cradle preparatory to the dramatic sawing off episode is a complicated, laborious and expensive proposition. When carefully and thoroughly done, however, it is a reasonably safe and sure method for launching a ship. In Essex it was always used for the larger and heavier ships or for a launching likely to receive considerable publicity and consequently attract a large crowd. Unfortunately, economics and human frailty being what they are, cradle launchings were not always carried through with care and thoroughness, giving rise to several nearly tragic accidents and much costly work to right the damage.

Most accidents occurred by reason of the fact that both way ends were not severed at the same instant. To illustrate, the ways that form the track are known as ground ways. The runners of the sled or cradle are called sliding ways. Before launching, in order to keep the boat from going down before its time, the sliding ways are fastened to the ground ways with large bolts. When the time comes and the boat is all ready, the team of men I spoke of simply saw off the ends of the sliding ways behind these bolts and with nothing restraining her any more, the boat launches. The trick comes in sawing off each of these way ends at the same instant; thus a series of scratches or depth marks at which the men pause in their sawing in order to keep abreast of one another.

If one pair of men saw off their ways before the other, it means that that side of the cradle starts to slide first and the resulting twist or racking of the cradle will usually topple the boat. This is what happened on several memorable occasions in Essex history. For example on July 12, 1916 the three-masted schooner *Nat L. Gorton*, 225 gross tons, launching from A.D. Story's yard, had her cradle twist beneath her and over she went. The impact threw a lady guest over the side and the shape of the great hull on the side that hit the ground was noticeably changed. It took the efforts of the yard crew plus a gang of building movers several days to get her up and a new cradle built. An expensive proposition, to say the least. Another vessel, the schooner *Mary F. Curtis*, 121 gross tons, fell over in the James & Tarr yard on September 11, 1903. On that occasion nearly 100 people were on board. Surprisingly, it seems, no one was severely hurt.

The launching process was fraught with all sorts of hazards to bedevil the poor shipbuilder. Not the least of these was the very river itself that was about half big enough to receive the size of the vessels launched into it. The wonder is that many more accidents didn't happen. Many times a vessel, plunging over the bank into relatively shallow water near the shore would dip her keel into the mud and fetch up then and there half in and half out of the water. What a mess that was. If a waiting tug couldn't budge her or a higher tide couldn't float her off, the gang must go down into the muck at low tide and try to rig a new ways. That all their efforts were ultimately successful is attested by the fact that all the boats are gone. None have remained.

Launching incidents sometimes took a rather bizarre turn. The jokesters tell us of the boat which, when she launched, kept on going—right to the bottom.

A launching accident caused a three-master schooner *Nat L. Gordon* to roll on the ways.

We had one once that did just that. She leaked so badly from having dried out in the sun that shortly after hitting the water she disappeared beneath the waves. Again, while it was not uncommon for a boat to roll down in hitting the water, the schooner *Radio* in December 1923, and by a quirk of design, rolled down and stayed there, part way over on her beam ends. In 1911 the wife of the skipper and namesake of the new schooner *Flora L. Oliver* waved as they slid down the ways and then as the vessel took the plunge, took one herself—right over the rail. This also was in December.

An interesting story is told of how what might have been a melancholy episode was averted by some prudent forethought. The schooner *Richard* was nearly completed at the time the firm of Oxner and Story failed. The vessel sat there for a year or so before disposition by the receivers in August of 1907. Her seams were wide open and to launch her in that condition was certainly risky, so help was enlisted from one of the Essex fire companies. The men of Essex No. 2 responded with their hand tub and squirted water into her hold until the planks were sufficiently swelled to be safe. The boat was launched without further incident and pursued a successful career.

There was, as I said, a second method of launching, used in Essex, whereby instead of a so-called cradle, the vessel was leaned over onto a single way and skated into the water on her own keel and one bilge. I have never heard of its being done in this way anywhere else, though, of course, it may have been. This method was by far the most popular among Essex builders since it was less work and consequently less expensive to perform and since it had the added advantage of putting the boat in the position of entering the water almost on her beam ends. By so doing she drew less water near the shallow banks and then by the time she righted up she was into the deep water at the middle of the river. Also to be considered was the fact that afterward there was very little trash to be fished out of the water. A cradle, on the other hand, carried a tremendous amount of lumber into the drink along with the boat, much of which was smashed and all of which had to be retrieved.

A side launching, as we called it, was very spectacular to watch and even more exciting perhaps was the process of knocking out the blocks. A vessel ready to launch would have a ground way built up under the turn of the bilge on one side only. Beneath the keel and between the blockings on which the boat had been built were placed a series of greased wooden slabs. By means of a series of large screw jacks the ship was then leaned over onto the ways. Now, as the men split away the supporting blocks, the keel came to rest instead on the greased slabs. When enough of the blocks were split out, she started to move. This is where the tension and excitement came in.

They started from aft and worked forward splitting out each block as they came to it. As they worked near the bow, the vessel would give a noticeable quiver with each successive block split away. Finally with perhaps five or six left to go it could be seen that she was beginning to inch her way down. Suddenly, as the men attacked another block, would come a loud crack and a groan and the vessel was on her way. The men would leap clear, the sponsor smashed her bottle, and all stood with bated breath for the plunge. It was very exciting. You never knew quite what to expect.

Sometimes a vessel started when hardly more than half the blocks were out. Other times they would go to the very last one before she moved. Worse yet was the boat, which continued just to sit there when all the blocks were gone. First they would try to start it with a couple of jacks. If that was no good, the tug would put its hawser aboard and pull. Usually one or the other or a combination of tug and jacks would do it, though not always. In that event the vessel had to be secured and the ways taken apart and regreased. Then, on another day, they would try all over again. "The joys of a shipbuilder's life," my father used to say, even if on occasion he did treat the whole business in somewhat of a devil-may-care, let's-have-a-good-time spirit. I like the account of how he and the Burnham brothers, Perry and Alden, came out of the club one night. A warm summertime full moon bathed the landscape in a brilliant light and it seemed a shame to waste it by going home to bed.

"Let's go down to the yard and launch that vessel that's ready," said Father.

"Why not?" said the other two. "Let's go."

So down they went. The tide was nearly high and all they needed to do was knock out the keel blocks, so they pitched in and began to split.

At length they reached the crucial block and the vessel began to slide. The men jumped clear and almost at once a thick cloud obscured the moon and all became black as pitch. They heard her groan and heard her take the plunge, but not a thing could they see. At length came a mighty crash as the vessel, innocent of any restraining lines, met the wharf on the opposite shore.

"Well, there isn't much we can do now," said Father and without further ado the three men went home to bed. No lines, no nothing. In the morning there she was, drifting peacefully about the river basin, but the rudder was smashed to smithereens.

In the later days as newspaper publicity about the launchings became more prevalent, a kind of holiday or carnival atmosphere grew up around the event. Owners began to deck out their boats with strings of flags and bunting and the crowds got bigger and bigger. Ordinary ship-carpenters suddenly found themselves the star actors in a very exciting drama. Some of them would even "ham it up" a teenier bit. It was fun to give the crowd a good show.

There was a kind of ritual to the whole business. Most preparations were made in the days immediately preceding a scheduled launch. It was generally best to plan the event for a time when the tide was high somewhere near the middle of the day. That gave time for last minute preparations and then time to get straightened out afterward. The weather was anxiously watched especially in regard to wind direction since an easterly wind made it difficult if not impossible for the tug to cross the bar at the mouth of our river. The presence of the tug was necessary since Essex ships were always towed to Gloucester or Boston to have the spars, rigging, and/or machinery installed. It was difficult and dangerous to leave a large vessel moored in the river basin after launching.

If the weather, therefore, looked favorable on the appointed day, the procedure began as the tide rose. The actual freeing of the ship by removing her blocks never started, though, unless the tug had actually been sighted on the way. If, then, came the cry, "Towboat's coming" the launching began.

The sponsor and her large bottle of "booze" never failed to evoke much merriment and jesting and two or three could always be counted on to dive with outstretched caps for the tantalizing torrent. Occasionally the friction of the heavy vessel would set the grease afire which created another scramble to put out the flames. Lastly, everyone must look out for the drag.

The drag was a huge bundle of heavy timbers weighing sometimes several tons, bound up with a chain and fastened to the boat with a long and tremendously large hawser. Its purpose was to check the momentum of the vessel once she was overboard. Most of the hawser was coiled on the ground and payed out as the ship went down the ways. Then as the bitter end was reached, the great line went taut and the drag took off with a roar. Slam bang it went along the ground pulverizing anything that might remain in its way. Seeing it go was almost as good as the launching itself. Sometimes, however, it did catch on something and then with a report like a cannon, the mighty hawser would bust and the ends came whistling through the air like some outlandish demon. It was all very satisfying and the crowd usually went home knowing they'd seen something.

If it were one of the beautiful racers being launched there was always the additional spectacle of a large group of dignitaries or celebrities in attendance. Sometimes they even closed the schools so that the children might attend. The last such occasion was the launching from A. 0. Story's yard of the *Gertrude L. Thebaud* on March 17, 1930. In April 1921 over eight thousand spectators lined the little causeway between Essex and South Essex to watch the schooner *Mayflower* take her maiden dip. This was a greater throng than came to see Cal Coolidge when he visited town in 1926.

In the summer or when the weather was pleasant and warm a great treat for many Essex folks was to climb aboard a newly launched schooner and go around to Gloucester aboard her. As soon as the new ship had been picked up by the tug and remnants of the launching cleared away, she was brought alongside the little wharf ostensibly to pick up the owner and his party. However, anybody who wanted to could usually clamber aboard and enjoy a delightful excursion down the river and across the bay. It was an occasion of great sociability. Often the decks would be crowded with young and old, gaily togged out and carrying picnic baskets and hampers with all sorts of goodies. If the boat was towed all the way out around Cape Ann so much the better, although many oft-times wished they'd left their goodies alone. It was apt to get a little rough out there. Upon arrival in Gloucester all would troop up town and come home on the electrics. A good time was had by all.

There have been many occasions when very wealthy men have had their yachts built in Essex. This often meant that the launching would be embellished with a fine collation complete with caterer and once even a bagpipe band. One of these yachts was towed clear to Boston after launching and an enthusiastic group of the owner's young friends went along for the ride. There were plenty of high spirits, liquid and otherwise, among the group and the party got more and more lively. As things turned out, the boat leaked a little and by the time they were off Nahant the water was fairly deep in the hold. Undismayed by this turn of events the young people stripped off their clothes and the hold of the boat became a delightful swimming pool with all hands gaily splashing about as they sailed along. Upon arrival in Boston (the boat didn't sink) they gratefully presented our local river pilot, Mr. Thales Cook, with two quarts of fine Scotch. Since these were Prohibition days and since Mr. Cook was a man to appreciate a gift so fine, he carefully stowed them under his coat and started for the North Station whence he could catch a train for Essex. Fortune was not to smile on Thales, however, for as he was crossing the broad reaches of the main concourse in the station one of the precious bottles slipped from its hiding place and fell to the floor with a resounding crash. Without so much as a sidelong glance or even breaking his stride, Thales made for the platform and leaped aboard the 4:35 and soon was safely on his way.

That it was possible for the weather to have a vital influence on the economic life of the town was dramatically illustrated during the 1880's. There came an unusually severe winter one year which caused the river ice to grow to an extraordinary depth. The shipyards of the town had been very busy and it wasn't long before several vessels stood ready for launching. However, because of the ice no tug could come into the river to get them, nor yet was it even possible to launch them. The situation got worse as boat after boat was completed and then just sat there. New ones couldn't be started because there simply wasn't room in the yards. It finally reached a point where all work practically closed and hardship was prevalent among the men. Furthermore it also made things bad in Gloucester since at this particular time there was considerable need for the new boats.

At length the various builders decided something must be done and soon. To this end they co-operated in hiring a group to dynamite the river ice. It was quite a thing. People talked about the dynamiting for years afterward. It became one of those events from which people reckoned or remembered time. "Let's see," someone might say, "I think Cousin Emma was married the summer after they dynamited the river." It worked, though, and with the help, I suppose, of flood tides and a break in the weather the "boat jam" was eventually alleviated.

The last of the big three-masted schooners to be built in Essex was started by my father in 1921 in the boom following World War I. This vessel was built on

Ice was thick on the Essex River in the winter of 1901. Shown in the yard of James and Tarr.

speculation and was destined to sit on the ways for eight years before she launched. Named the *Adams* after Mother's family, she was a victim of the bust which came soon after, and Father just stopped work and let her sit there. Occupying a berth next to the main street with her great bowsprit sticking out over the road, she soon became a landmark the country around. People everywhere talked about her and tourists stopped summer after summer to look again at this curiosity. At length her sister ship, the *Lincoln*, launched in 1919, was rammed by a steamer and Father decided to finish and launch the *Adams*.

The launching was scheduled for April 13, 1929 and as the day drew near the excitement grew. A vessel this size (she was about 165 feet long) hadn't been launched in a long while and might never be again. The papers heard of it and all sorts of people called our house. My mother took 99 phone calls before she stopped counting. The day came and with it a northeast snowstorm. Things had progressed so far that Father decided to go ahead anyway, and so at high tide, before the anxious eyes of most of the town and many from outside, the *Adams*

The schooner *Adams* was an Essex landmark for eight years. She stood with bowsprit out over Main Street and was found to have a hive of bees between her planking and ceiling. The *Adams* was the last wooden coasting steamer to be built in the U.S.

slid into the river. Many felt that since she had sat there so long, she would be reluctant to leave, but luckily the launching went well, although she had to remain tied in the river basin for two or three days waiting for the tugs. When they finally were able to come, it took two tugs two days to get her to Gloucester. I am sure that the strain of looking after the vessel as she was buffeted by gales and flood tides straining at her lines there in the little river took years off Father's life.

After the incident in 1916 when the *Nat L. Gorton* fell down in launching, my mother would never again go near the shipyard at the time of a boat-launch. We had a friend, Miss Alice Porter Burnham, who lived just across the creek and who could see every launching in our yard from her back piazza. She agreed after that to call Mother on the telephone as soon as a boat was safely in the water and let her know that everything was all right. I can still remember, as a young boy, when unable, perhaps from sickness, to attend a launching, of hearing the tug's whistle and then the ring of the telephone as Alice Porter called to give the word to Mother.

So you can imagine, perhaps, the work and worry as well as the thrills that went with launching the ships, particularly when you consider that since 1790 there have been over 3,300 launchings in Essex. Luckily there were men who could take it lightly and all in a day's work, as for example our friend John Prince. When he was well into his eighties someone asked him once how he launched "those big vessels over on their sides like that." "Why, that's nothing," said John. "I'd launch 'em on a shingle if I had a good foundation!"

six

The Burnhams

LATTER-DAY DEVELOPMENTS IN THE arts and practices of publicity have perhaps attributed to the Storys and James's more than their rightful share of credit for the long and excellent reputation of Essex ships and shipbuilders. It pains me, for example, to recall that the only Essex ship I ever heard of to sink after she launched was built by a Story.

To give credit where credit is due, one must acknowledge the tremendous part played by the Burnham's in the record of Essex shipbuilding. As mentioned, local tradition has always held that the very first boat to be built here was built by a Burnham. From that start an astonishing number of Burnham's engaged themselves in vessel building, some achieving considerable prominence not only as builders but also as sea-faring men. Just for fun I am going to enumerate the Burnhams who became shipbuilders merely from 1815 on.

Aaron Burnham 2nd, America Burnham, Benjamin Burnham 2nd, Daniel Burnham, Ebenezer Burnham, Eli F. Burnham, Gilman M. Burnham, Issacher Burnham, Jacob Burnham 2nd, Jeremiah Burnham, John S. Burnham, Luke Burnham, Michael Burnham, Moses Burnham 3rd, Nathan Burnham, Nathan Burnham 3rd, Noah Burnham, Oliver Burnham, Parker Burnham, Parker Burnham 2nd, Samuel Burnham, Willard R. Burnham, Willard A. Burnham and Zaccheus Burnham. Twenty-four of them, and judging by the names, they certainly were Bible readers as well as boat builders.

Just as a matter of academic interest, here are the Storys who built vessels during the same period: Abel Story, Andrew Story, Arthur D. Story, Dana Story, David Story, Epes Story, Ephraim Story 2nd, George M. Story, Jacob Story (earlier), Jacob Story (later), Job Story, John P. Story, Jonathan Story, Jonathan Story 3rd, Joseph Story, Michael Story 2nd, Perkins Story and Samuel Story. Only eighteen of these.

How many Burnhams (or even Storys) were engaged in ship building before 1815 is virtually impossible to tell, although with Burnham being the most numerous of Essex family names throughout our history, there were doubtless many more. In any case, the Burnham reputation for quality of boat and workmanship was always high.

Obviously limitations of space and of reader interest do not permit an account of each of these Burnhams, but a few words about several of the more outstanding would, I think, be of interest.

The man who, among the Burnhams led perhaps the most eventful life, was Captain Parker Burnham 2nd, born in Chebacco Parish September 18, 1781 and died there just 90 years later. He was the son of Enoch and Hannah (Bennett) Burnham. Little appears to be known of his early years except that as a young man he evidently entered the shipbuilding business in what had been the shipyard of his uncle, the first Mr. Parker Burnham. This was in the north part of town at what is now called Hardy's Point. We do know, however, that he married Mary Hardy on September 14, 1809.

In 1811 Mr. Burnham built the largest square-sterned vessel that had ever been constructed in Chebacco prior to the War of 1812. This was a 220-ton brig called the *Silk Worm*. One would certainly be amazed on seeing the little creek that now flows past the site of Mr. Burnham's shipyard to think that a vessel of such size could ever have been launched into so small a body of water.

With the completion of this brig, Parker Burnham now became a mariner, first sailing for five years as master of his own *Silk Worm*. He made many voyages to Lisbon and to various ports in the Mediterranean, sailing in the employ of the Sargents and other prominent merchants of Boston. History relates that he became one of the most skillful and trusted navigators of his time and that while experiencing many terrific gales he never was shipwrecked nor did he suffer disaster of any kind. It was said that he would never take chances at sea, and if a storm threatened would always give orders to shorten sail in order that the ship might be adequately prepared.

Capt. Burnham's retirement from the sea was hastened somewhat by a rather singular circumstance. To read from the record we find that he became weary of life on the ocean and had about concluded to stay ashore and become a landsman again. Yielding, however, to the entreaties of his employers, he at length decided to go on one more voyage. He therefore sent his sea chest aboard and was waiting only for a fair wind to cast off. As he entered his cabin, however, he felt a sudden presentiment that if he sailed he would never return. The feeling grew so strong that he went back to the ship owners and cancelled his engagement. They procured another captain who sailed away and according to the story, crew and ship were never heard from again.

As he had felt he should do, Capt Burnham returned to Chebacco, since become Essex, and resumed a shipbuilding and business career, which he followed the rest of his life. Along with his ships, he was long remembered, as I mentioned, earlier, for his discontinuance of the use of rum in his yard; also for his speedy construction of the pinky schooner *July*.

Perhaps even more remarkable than all these things was the fact that Capt. Burnham never worried about his affairs or his business losses, nor did they ever, as he said, deprive him of a night's sleep. He once sold a new vessel entirely on credit to the apparently prosperous Boston firm of Coolidge, Head and Poor. Soon after taking delivery, the firm made a disastrous failure, with Capt. Burnham losing the entire price of the boat, amounting to several thousands of dollars. In order to see if anything might be recovered the captain hitched his new horse to his carriage and off they went to Boston. All proved to be lost, however, and, to cap the climax, as he reached Salem on the way home, the new horse dropped dead.

"What luck?" they asked him when at length he reached home.

Replied Capt. Burnham, "Coolidge, Head and Poor old horse have all gone together!"

I have alluded to the fact that the great proportion of Gloucester ships were built in Essex yards. Not only did Essex builders construct the Gloucester vessels, in many cases they were also instrumental in financing them. In the middle 1800's as the fishing industry in Gloucester began to grow more rapidly and to prosper, and before the day when commercial banks began the more modem methods of financing, it was the Essex builders who many times made it possible for the Gloucester firms to acquire fleets of new vessels. The following little story illustrates the way this was done and provides a glimpse of another of our shipbuilding Burnhams.

It seems that in 1860 Mr. Sylvanus Smith of Gloucester had recently associated himself with Capt. Joseph Rowe to form the fishing firm of Smith and Rowe.

The two men came to Essex to inquire about buying a vessel and found upon their arrival that Mr. Luke Burnham had one already built which would meet their requirements. They concluded an agreement with Mr. Burnham in the manner customary to the period, wherein they agreed to purchase the boat for a price of $60 per carpenter ton, it being expected that the boat would measure out about 95 tons. Payment was to be in four equal amounts; one quarter down and one quarter in each of three annual installments.

The new boat was launched and towed to Gloucester where her spars and rigging were installed and other outfit put aboard. She was also measured by the district customhouse, which found her tonnage to be somewhat more than the expected 95. As soon as she was ready for sea, Mr. Burnham came down in order to pass the papers of the sale and to conclude the business arrangements. As he seated himself in the office, the partners handed him a check for $5700, the full price of the vessel.

"What's this?" said Mr. Burnham.

"Why, the full amount of the price."

In anger he threw the check upon the table saying.

"I won't take it! It is not according to our agreement and besides, you are only paying me $60 a ton for 95 tons. The vessel measures several tons more and now you are paying me the whole thing at one payment, which was not agreed!"

Although flattered that their notes were better than their cash, Mr. Smith and Mr. Rowe could not make Luke Burnham change his mind. He explained that by having his payments come annually he could arrange his own affairs more satisfactorily and that if they were to do business with him, things would be carried out strictly according to agreement.

As a postscript it might be added that Smith and Rowe had two more vessels built in Essex, these by Mr. Aaron Burnham who is remembered as having finished his career by building 22 vessels in 22 months, only to go broke in doing it.

An Essex man through and through was Willard Alvin Burnham, a man whose father was a Burnham, whose mother was an Andrews and whose wife was a Story! Born in Essex in October 1841, he began working in his father's shipyard when seventeen years old. To distinguish him from the older Burnham whose name was Willard R., he came to be called, as was the Essex custom, by his first two names and was known to all until the day he died in 1918 as Willard Alvin.

At the outbreak of the Civil War, Willard Alvin went to work first in the naval shipyard at Charlestown, Massachusetts, and then at the one in Kittery, Maine. It was here that he was employed in the construction of the famous U. S. man-of-war *Kearsage* which subsequently sank the Confederate privateer *Alabama*.

In 1871 he established a shipyard in Gloucester in company with Mr. Daniel Poland, but after a few years they gave up this business and Mr. Burnham returned to Essex. Here he engaged in shipbuilding on his own account, doing business near what had been his father's yard in South Essex. He carried on the business, building many fine vessels until his retirement in 1893. At that time, it will be remembered, the Democrats under Grover Cleveland went back into power and Mr. Burnham, a staunch Republican of the old school, said that the country would most certainly go to pot. That being the case, there was certainly no point in continuing to do business, so therefore he quit. Some, however, felt that his real reason was an unwillingness to install some of the newer steam machinery.

Willard Alvin did not retire from civic affairs but took the opportunity to serve in the legislature and later as a member of the Essex board of selectmen, an assessor, an overseer of the poor, a member of the school committee, a trustee of the public library and an officer of the fire department. In addition, he was active in the Masons and Knights of Pythias, as well as several local political organizations. In short, he was what might be described as a good solid citizen and a Burnham who could and did further the name and reputation of Essex.

We have talked about shipbuilding Burnhams. The men of this name who followed other pursuits and distinguished themselves and Essex while doing so are legion. That, however, is something we will have to leave for another occasion.

seven

Arthur D. Story

"Georgie! I want you to go to Manch'ster and get a man." That's all he said, whereupon he turned and walked off, giving his attention to something else. A.D. Story was not a man to use ten words where five words would do. "Georgie," being a man of more than ordinary common sense and perception, knew that no more directions would be forthcoming from old A.D., so without a word he went over and getting into A.D's car, started for the neighboring town of Manchester. As he drove along he reasoned that probably the depot would be the best place to start looking, so, as he approached the station platform, there, sure enough, was a man standing expectantly with briefcase in hand. Drawing alongside and rolling down the window Georgie called out,

"Say, would you be the feller wanting to go over to Story's in Essex?"

"Why yes," said the man with a look of surprise.

"Well, hop in," said Georgie, "and let's get started."

Perhaps because he knew Georgie would use his head and not ask too many questions, A.D. often singled him out for errands of this kind and somehow Georgie always got the message. Georgie, or more properly George Story, no relation to A.D., worked as a caulker in the Story shipyard for many years. A.D. might say,

"One of these days, Georgie, I want you to caulk around that rudder post." From experience Georgie knew that "one of these days" meant within the next two hours or there would be hell to pay.

Mr. A. D. Story, builder, stands under the bow of the racing schooner *Columbia* in 1923.

Arthur D. Story was hardly an ordinary man in any sense of the word. First of all he stood 6 feet 1½ inches in his stocking feet and, in his prime, weighed 215 lbs. He had coal black hair, which was still there and still quite dark when he died at 77. When I was 10 years old and he was 74, he could beat me easily in a foot race from the barn to the back door. His face, while not perhaps handsome, reflected a determined yet benevolent character and was accentuated by a somewhat large "Roman" nose. He never wore an overcoat around the shipyards, just a heavy sweater under a suit coat even in the coldest weather. Once in a while he could be seen to blow his nose on his mitten.

As a younger man he was possessed of great physical strength and years after his death some of the things he did were living legend in the minds of those who remembered him. Time and again I have heard the stories of how he would help carry the great oaken deck beams up the brow to the high staging. He alone would carry one end while sometimes three men would carry the other. A man who tried to match him at this feat once succeeded, but as the story goes, never worked again. He could flip over long oak planks merely by bracing one foot against the lower edge and then by giving a little tug with one hand on the other edge, over they'd go.

Perhaps as well known as his perpetual buttonhole bouquet and the cigar that was never lit was his reputation for directness and brevity. There was a kind of plainspoken forthrightness about him that excited the admiration of those too timid perhaps to practice themselves, but for those to whom his remarks were directed, a better word for this quality was "blunt." He came out of church one Sunday morning and as the minister standing in the doorway offered his hand in the usual parting pleasantry he said simply,

"You talked too long!"

A gushing female rushed up to him once amid the last minute press of launching preparations and asked,

"When are you going to launch, Mr. Story?" Without even looking around the reply came, "When we're ready."

I remember once as a small boy I came into the house on a warm spring afternoon and complained to "Pa" (Mother was away at the time) that I was awful hot in my long winter underwear.

"Well, boy," he said, "go take it off and bring it here." I did as I was told, whereupon Pa reached into his pocket and taking out his trusty jack-knife proceeded to make short sleeves and legs out of long ones. Mother sputtered about it for weeks.

"Imagine," she said, "spoiling a perfectly good set of underwear with a fool trick like that."

In somewhat the same vein as the Frenchman who said of Father, "I deen' speak to heem and he deen' answer me," was the experience of Mr. George McIntire who was quite a local business man himself in his younger days. During the months of the First World War when business in the shipyards was booming, Mr. McIntire had cut and milled out a fine lot of white pine boards from one of his woodlots. He inquired of his neighbor, Mr. Fon Knowlton, where he might dispose of the boards.

"Why," said Mr. Knowlton, "I think Arthur could use those boards. I'll speak to him about it if I see him tomorrow or next day."

In a few days Fon came back to Mr. McIntire to say that Arthur could indeed use the boards and to send them over if he wanted to. So Mr. McIntire loaded them on his wagon, brought them over and dumped them off under Father's watchful eye. A week or so later he made out and sent his bill and was subsequently paid without ever so much as a word being exchanged between them regarding the boards.

It was the custom, since most other business was done there anyway, for Essex shipbuilders to do their banking in Gloucester. It was Father's habit to drive down in his buggy (and later his car) every Saturday morning to get the payroll and to make such other business calls as were necessary. His bank, The Gloucester Safe Deposit and Trust Company, was located right in the square at the center of the city. Directly across the narrow main street was the post office, which sat up rather high and had a broad flight of wooden steps in the front. These steps provided a gathering place in good weather for vessel captains and other seafaring men to gossip and observe the passing scene.

As the story goes, Father was about to enter the Trust Company one morning when a captain, sitting across on the post office steps spied him and hollered over to say that he wanted a new vessel like the one so-and-so had. Acknowledging the order with a wave and a brief word or two to reply, Father continued on into the bank. In due course the vessel was built and paid for. Nothing more seemed necessary.

There was also the time Captain Joe Mesquita came into the yard to talk with Father about having a boat built. They sat on a plank under the tree and discussed briefly what he wanted. Presently the Captain inquired about a contract. Without a word Father reached over and selecting a large broad chip he wrote on it with his pencil,

"I agree to build and Captain Joe Mesquita agrees to pay for a vessel of about 65 tons."
Signed: Arthur D. Story
Captain Joe Mesquita

That was the contract!

There was another Portuguese captain who, while not particularly concerned with the contractual aspects of his business dealings with Father, was mostly concerned with his desire for a well constructed boat. His command of English was not too good and after struggling to tell Father how he wanted things, finally gave up with the remark,

"Please, just do me good, Mr. Story."

Father could not always have been a man of such few words since he was active in Republican politics for many years. He served in the Massachusetts legislature for two terms and was a member of the Massachusetts Electoral College, which in January 1901 cast its votes for William McKinley and Theodore Roosevelt. I was always impressed as I looked at the picture of this august body that in a day of beards and walrus mustaches, Father was the only one in the group of 14 who was clean shaven. And speaking of pictures, I well remember that T. R. was one of Father's heroes and his large framed picture hung for years in our living room beside the tall clock.

In June 1896, Father had been a delegate to the Republican National Convention, which met in St. Louis. At that time he was a supporter of Thomas B. Reed of Maine and opposed the nomination of William McKinley. An interesting clipping from a Boston paper of the period tells of a lively fracas, which took place one midnight during the convention in the Southern Hotel of St. Louis. Various delegations from New England were staging a parade and demonstration for their man, Mr. Reed, when they were set upon by a group of McKinley men. To quote the clipping of the Boston "Journal":

"Immediately there was a great crush. Two score big Massachusetts men rushed to the rescue. Big Representative Story of Essex, without hesitation, marched up to the McKinley crowd, which was engaged in the work of devastation, and rushing through them swung them right and left like a locomotive snowplow. He grasped a man in each hand and swung him around like a torch." A delightful donneybrook ensued and to quote again from the last sentence, "- - and Representative Story, his nose somewhat scarred, but otherwise unscratched, looked like a radiant victor crowned with wild olives."

The old scrapbook contains many articles demonstrating Father's enthusiasm for local and state politics. He would appear to have been something of a stormy petrel and a thorn in the side of the regional "machine". Between his terms in the legislature (the first in 1896, the second in 1910) he sought the Republican nomination for state senator. He didn't make it, but I never knew whether he was defeated or withdrew from the race. At any rate, judging by the clippings, he had a fine time trying and what's more, he made quite a goodly number of speeches.

By now the reader may have become aware that it has been necessary for me to gather a good part of the information concerning my own father from clippings and from the reminiscences of those who had remembered him. It was interesting (and amusing to some) that I was born in Father's 65th year. While I was the tenth child, I was Mother's only child, the first Mrs. Story having died some years before. To further confuse the family picture, my half-brothers and half-sisters were well old enough to be my parents and were in fact contemporaries more or less of my mother, having grown up and gone to school with her. With two exceptions, my nieces and nephews were all older than myself. Father died just before my 13th birthday so that my own recollections of him, while extremely vivid, were necessarily limited in scope.

More than once, when, as a little boy, I accompanied Father on a business trip to Boston or Gloucester, a chance acquaintance who Father hadn't seen for some years would come over and pat my head saying, "My, my, young man, aren't you having a good time traveling around with Grandpa this morning." Pa and I would exchange broad grins and I would say, "That ain't my grandpa, that's my father!" Inevitably a hearty laugh ensued and Father would be warmly congratulated.

We might do well before going further to begin at the beginning. Arthur Dana Story was born in Essex on October 11, 1854, the first of Job and Lucinda (Brown) Story's fourteen children. Job was a shipbuilder as had been his father, Abel. The family home was one-half of a large house in the very center of town. The other half of the house was occupied by Job's half-brother Newton.

One of his early jobs was taking care of a neighbor's cows and driving them to and from the pasture. The hard-scrabble life of the country town in those days was not completely without its sport and fun, for I remember hearing Father tell of the occasion when, as a youngster, he was coasting one winter day with some of his friends. With their little wooden sleds they would slide down the slopes of the shore and out onto the treacherous salt ice of the river. It was Father's fortune to drop through a hole, sled and all. Then, incredibly, he was carried along by the current under the ice only to come up through another hole. The sled, however, was gone until the following spring when someone picked it off the bank far down the river. On another occasion, this time in the summer, they were swimming, as was their habit, from the gristmill locks by a drawbridge. Father dove and gouged his stomach on a submerged projection. The first aid treatment for the wound was the application of cobwebs from under the bridge to stop the bleeding.

His energies as a chore-boy and his diligence in school were rewarded in 1871 with his entry into Phillips Academy at Andover. He was very happy here and from all I know did well, but one year was all that could be managed and Father returned to Essex. Thus in 1872, at the age of eighteen, he took up the family business of shipbuilding, forming a partnership with an older man, Mr. Moses Adams, also of Essex.

Beginning with the 72-gross-ton schooner *S. R. Lane*, they built twenty vessels in the next eight years. On one occasion during that period in 1879, when business was dull, he went to work for his father, Job, helping to build a large three-master. The wages paid on this job were $2.00 per day. On another occasion when the vessel-building picture was none too bright, Father took the examinations for the Boston police force. Evidently he thought better of it afterwards, for nothing ever came of it.

In 1880 the firm of Adams and Story "failed up", as they used to say, and each man went into business for himself. Father's first vessel on his own was the schooner *Aroostook*, also 72 gross tons, built that summer on Corporation wharf. For reasons which no one seemed to recollect, his next one, the *Richard Lester*, was set up in a yard across the river from the wharf while the frames, curiously, were made on the wharf, then slid overboard, floated across, and finally erected on the vessel's keel. Interesting, but it must have involved a lot of extra work. Since Father was hiring both spots, it was likely that a question of space or rent was involved.

In the realm of pure statistics it can be noted that Arthur D. Story went on from these humble and rather modest beginnings to build before his death in 1932 a total of 425 ships having a gross tonnage of more than 45,000; an average of over seven vessels a year and 106 gross tons apiece. In one year alone, 1901, he launched 18 vessels for a total of 1941 gross tons. That averages out to a 108 ton ship every three weeks. In the spring of that year there were nine vessels on the ways at once. This was accomplished with a work force of no more than 65 men at any one time and with only one steam powered band saw and treenail (trunel) lathe. The saw was used in getting out the frames and planks; all other operations were performed strictly by hand, one piece at a time. I have never taken the trouble to look up comparative statistics— it's not important—but I would call the record fairly impressive. As far as Essex was concerned, it was never equaled by any other individual.

It is of further interest to see that shipbuilding was only the principal concern of A.D. Story. From time to time he acquired numerous business sidelines in addition to the shipyard. He owned and rented seven houses in Essex besides the one he lived in; an eighth house was in the next town of Hamilton. He owned the store occupied for many years by the A&P and a 180 acre farm, having on it one of the largest and loveliest historic houses of the town. At various times he owned a grocery store, had a major interest in several blacksmith shops, a fish market, and a yacht yard, was a Director of two banks, and in 1914, when vessel building was slow, he had some of his gang building a bowling alley which he operated for several years. This, incidentally, was the building later to become the first Roman Catholic Church in Essex.

In addition to all these, he was, by virtue of not having been paid in full, the part owner of numerous fishing vessels. It was the custom in such a case for the builder to take a number of shares to equal his unpaid balance and to hold them until they could be bought by whomever had contracted for the vessel. All too often, however, what happened was that the builder just got stuck for these shares and never did realize anything on them.

Sometimes, instead of shares, a builder would take a preferred mortgage on the vessel in lieu of his money, but here again the result was often the same. Father's estate would have been twice as big if all his vessel holdings could have been capitalized. He did, however, build several large vessels to his own account and operated them for many years. His last were two large three-masted coasting schooners that carried bulk cargoes, mostly coal and lumber, between the Maritime Provinces of Canada and Boston or New York.

Both these vessels were built from the same model. The first was the *Lincoln*, launched in April 1919. She ran successfully for nine years until being struck by a steamer in the fog. In spite of a huge gash amidships, which ran from the rail almost to the keel, she remained afloat, thanks to a hold solid full of lumber. She was literally one big block of wood. She limped into Gloucester where her cargo was discharged and her spars, rigging and sails were salvaged.

At this point Father decided to finish up and commission the *Adams*, which he had started on speculation in the boom of 1921. He had passed up a golden opportunity to sell her before the bubble burst and then was left with a 165 foot hull on his hands. For a time she was inhabited by a swarm of bees and when she finally launched in a northeast gale and snowstorm on April 13, 1929, she must have carried a good many pounds of honey along with her. (See also reference to *Adams* in chapter on Launchings.)

Because of the storm, the vessel had to be moored in the basin awaiting the arrival of the tug. Lines were strung off to trees and posts on shore—anything that seemed solid enough to hold. It was a difficult and trying experience in the teeth of the gale and flood tide. I can remember Father standing in the water near a point of land while he shouted orders to his men and struggled to do what he could to help. Suddenly who should appear on the scene but an insurance salesman who then and there started his pitch. I never knew Father's exact words, but they had a telling effect on that salesman who cleared out of there like a whipped dog.

A day or two later, when the vessel had finally arrived in Gloucester, Father piled some of the gang into his new Packard coupe to go down and finish up some work. The car was spotless for Mother had just cleaned it and had taken special pains with the windows. While not a smoker, Father did enjoy an occasional chew of crimp cut that he kept in the watch pocket of his pants. He was chewing some on this occasion and we hadn't gone far when it became necessary to do what all tobacco chewers do—spit. He let fly all over that nice clean rolled-up window and door. It had been so clean he couldn't even see the glass. How the crowd laughed.

I can well remember an occasion as a young boy going with Father to visit the *Adams* when she called at South Boston. I can especially remember the way the ship smelled as we sat at dinner in the big after cabin and the miserable tasting little canned peas that appeared on my plate. However, Captain Kelson was a genial host and did his best to make me feel at home. Following Father's death the *Adams* was sold to the swashbuckling Captain L. Mike Kennedy and, until her demise in a December Gulf Stream gale, she figured in several of his more hair-raising adventures.

For all of the years that A.D. Story carried on his multiple business enterprises there were only a few when he bothered with hiring a bookkeeper. Those were the days when government forms and income taxes as we know them were unheard of and nobody cared if a businessman kept minute and elaborate records. By and large his business was kept in his head and his checkbook.

At times when building was brisk and the gang was large, a man was hired to be a timekeeper and assist in preparation of the payroll. He would also make some effort at keeping records of a sort.

Usually, however, some members of the family did it. In late years it was my mother who put up the payroll and did it every Saturday without fail. She used to say that she could lie there dying, but if it came Saturday noon, she'd have to get up to put up that payroll.

The pay week ended on Friday night. After determining how much money he needed, Father would go to Gloucester to the bank every Saturday morning and bring home the cash. I should emphasize "every Saturday" because excepting the week of sickness just before he died and one other occasion when a heart attack felled him for a while in 1914, I think he went to Gloucester nearly every Saturday for fifty years. He would take the bundle of cash and the rolls of coin and casually drop them in his coat pocket, whereupon he went about the city attending to any errands he might have. Sometimes he might chuck the bundle into the little compartment just behind the driver's seat of our old Buick coupe. He never locked the car or even bothered to shut a window. For that matter, he never locked a door at home or anywhere. "You only lock your doors on the honest", he would say.

For all of the "R months" we had oyster stew at noon on Saturday after which Mother immediately prepared the envelopes for the men, packing them as she finished in an old brown suede satchel with fringe around it. It would then be my distinction together with any of my friends who happened to be in attendance, to go down to the yard with my Father and rush them around to the men.

Though always engrossed in his many business ventures and sometimes occupied with politics and political clubs, Arthur D. Story also found time for several social organizations. These consisted of membership in two lodges, the Oddfellows and the Knights of Pythias, and a local card-playing and recreational organization known as the 20th Century Club. Actually, it was this last that really seemed to interest him much since its membership was composed strictly of hometown friends and cronies who gathered evenings purely for the fun of it. It was the sort of institution that made no demands upon a man.

The oyster boats Benj. *M. Wallace* and *John A. Ericsson* in 1893. John Prince Story contracted for the labor on the *Benj. Wallace* for $950.00.

The one thing outside his business to which Father was deeply and conscientiously devoted was his church. His mother, a God fearing and dedicated New England Congregationalist, had brought him up in the church, and her influence was to stick with him always. Every Sunday of his life that found him able to stand on his two feet, also found him in church if it were at all possible to get there. He served on the Parish Committee of the Essex Congregational Church for years and years and was one of the most generous financial supporters the church ever had. Moreover Father attempted to carry his religion into his daily life as best he could. In spite of his brusque and outspoken manner, I don't believe I ever heard him speak mean or unkind words of anybody. He never swore or used dirty talk and under no circumstances would he conduct any of his business on Sunday. He was generous and forgiving almost to a fault. Any of his men, and many others too, could nearly always "touch" Arthur for a little loan when they felt they needed one. There were several in his business dealings who secured his trust and faith only to steal from him or cheat him shamefully in the end. I have been told of an occasion when a man who had once worked for him, upon meeting Father on the street in Gloucester, talked insultingly to him, cursing him and upbraiding him for some imaginary grievance. Father, realizing the man was drunk, said nothing and walked sadly away. A few days later and without having said a word, here was this same man going to work with the gang in the yard. "How come you put up with a thing like that, Arthur?" somebody asked. "Oh," said Father, "he was out of a job. He's got a family and needs the work." Paradoxically, for all his church going, Father steadfastly refused to "join the church" in the ecclesiastical sense of the word. Whenever anyone asked him why he would always reply, "I couldn't keep the promises."

Our house was a great Victorian monstrosity with a mansard roof that sat halfway up Winthrop Street. The outside was decorated with an abundance of "whirligigs" and "thingamajigs" which had been the height of fashion at the time the house was built. The inside was also impressive. Downstairs there were four large rooms, including the kitchen, dining room, silting room and parlor. There was also a tremendous front hall with stairway, a pantry off the kitchen, and a good sized back entry. Upstairs there were five bedrooms, a bathroom and another large hall. The rooms upstairs, by the way, were ten feet high while downstairs they were eleven! Plenty of space but not much convenience since in all those rooms there was about as much closet space as there is in a present-day bungalow. Furthermore the shape of the roof meant that the attic was only about four feet high at the most and since no stairway led to it, it was virtually useless for storage.

Father was of the school that believed that a man's home was his castle and that any and all jobs in or about the house were strictly the province of others besides himself. He sometimes alluded to the fact that he was supposed to have some Indian blood back along the line somewhere to which Mother would reply that she could believe that, since, as far as the housework was concerned, he figured she was no better than a squaw. She even tended the furnace, doing an excellent job of it, too, since she had been taught to build and keep a coal fire by her father, a locomotive engineer. As a matter of fact she became fiercely proud of her abilities as a fireman and would become extremely wroth with Father on the infrequent occasions when he had the temerity to tamper with her drafts, or worse yet, to shake the furnace without her specific instruction to do so. She was proud of the fact that one winter she shoveled sixteen tons of coal into that old Guerney, trying her best, as she said, "to heat this great ark of a place." She used to threaten that she was going down to the shipyard and have Ed Perkins make a stand six feet high for her armchair. Then when she finally got to sit down in the evening she'd "be up where all the heat is."

Besides the furnace, Mother kept a coal fire in the beautiful black iron "Fortess Crawford" we had in the kitchen. Since this fire was used to heat the hot water as well as for cooking, her kitchen fire never went out from one year to the next. Never mind how hot the weather got, the kitchen fire burned just the same. In cold weather seasons, for as long as he lived, there was always a large soapstone resting at the back of the kitchen stove that Father would wrap up in a gray flannel bag and take to bed with him when the time came. This was to keep his feet warm. It was also the custom at our house to use the coal fire in the kitchen stove to make toast. This we did by sticking the bread on a hand-made wrought-iron fork and holding it over the glowing coals. You had to remember, though, to get your toast made before you put more coal on. Nothing, I think, has yet been devised to replace the iron kitchen stove. Who can stick his feet in an electric oven or back up to one when he comes in cold and damp? Or where is the stove today on which you can put a chowder or a stew and have it simmer along all day?

From my standpoint as a boy the superior features of the old home were the dandy yard and better yet, the magnificent barn. First of all the yard, although really not very large, had, as was common at the turn of the century, quite a number of fruit trees. There were six or seven pear trees of various kinds, a plum tree, a quince bush, a crabapple tree, a regular apple tree bearing apples of an uncertain variety, two grape vines, a bed of raspberry bushes and a patch of rhubarb. Besides these we had two large lilac bushes, some bridal wreath and in the middle of the front lawn a lovely purple beech tree whose limbs came right down to the ground. This was unquestionably the best tree for climbing anybody ever saw and there was hardly a time when youngsters were about that there weren't at least two or three among its branches. The old apple tree was nice, too, because its limbs overhung the roof of the outdoor toilet and we could easily climb the framework of the high board fence that connected the house and the toilet and from the top of the fence to the roof was just a step. Then it was into the branches from the rooftop. The apple tree was where I built my tree hut. With all these things about the yard there was still room for Mother to have several flowerbeds and also space for a croquet set and an old-fashioned chair swing.

Our barn from a youngster's standpoint, was ideal for playing in. (I feel sorry for kids nowadays who have never known what it is to have a barn to play in.) This barn, if I may coin a phrase, was what one might call a "town barn" as distinct from a "farm barn." By this term I mean that the building was finely constructed after the fashion and architecture of the house and was designed primarily as a stable for several horses and a place to keep carriages or buggies. Such barns were extremely common years ago. Almost every suburban or even city home had one. It was the two-car garage of its day. Our barn had two floors, the upstairs being the hayloft and the lower floor divided into a larger section for the carriages with the smaller a stable having four stalls and a grain and harness room. By the time I came along the main section downstairs was then a garage with one of Father's old buggies stored over in a back corner. At that there was still ample room for a woodpile and two cars. The only occupant of the stables was old Jimmie, the shipyard draft horse. Because of him, however, we still used the harness room, and the hayloft was always partly filled with hay.

While I can remember Jimmie, a rather gentle red horse, and his predecessor, a villain known as "Old Red-eye", I don't recall Father's spirited driving horses which in years before had inhabited the stalls. He had one especially wild reddish beast that, I have been told by older residents who well remembered him, would take the bit in his teeth and run like the devil himself was in hot pursuit. This trait didn't bother Father much since he only seemed to do it when headed for home, and it made the trip a lot shorter. They said he could come the seven miles from Gloucester in a little over 20 minutes.

Father was not above a friendly race now and then if an opportunity arose and it arose one wintry day as Father and his light sleigh were approaching the top of Railroad Hill in West Gloucester on his way home to Essex. A shouted challenge and away they went down the hill toward the curve which disappeared beneath the railroad underpass.

Not too many minutes later the men in the yard looked up to see Father's red horse coming like the wind across the causeway from South Essex, bit in his teeth and trailing behind an empty pair of shafts. Sensing that something was amiss, Mr. O. Perry Burnham hitched up and started for Gloucester to look for Father. In due course he came upon a very sheepish looking A.D. Story plodding along the road with his robe over one arm.

It developed that the racers, as they came around the curve and under the railroad bridge had met a farm sled about to enter from the other side. One shaft of the heavy sled had gone right into the seat beside the spot where Father sat and over went the sleigh, Father and all. Out came the shafts of the sleigh and horse and empty shafts disappeared around the bend, leaving Father in the snow bank beside the road.

I would hesitate to guess how much of my early youth I spent playing in that barn. All the neighborhood kids played there with me and the number of games of hide-and-seek are beyond counting. The vacant stalls were sometimes piled with locust treenails from the shipyard and we could vary our amusement by climbing on them. Merely hurling ourselves about in the hay or jumping from the beams over head could always expend sheer exuberance. The more adventurous of my companions used to contrive to shinny up to the fine cupola that surmounted the barn and survey the world from this lofty perch. I might add that, true to tradition, the cupola was itself ornamented with the familiar galloping horse weathervane complete with holes punctured by shots from a Daisy air rifle.

And so we picture the yard, the barn, the well with its wooden pump, the purple beech tree, the pear trees, the high board fence, and, the outdoor privy; things common to most yards then, but such wonderful times we had there. Tag, scrub, hide-and-seek, Quaker meeting, red light, hopscotch, marbles and many others were games we played day after day. We even had a miniature firemen's muster once. Isn't it too bad that kids have to grow up and relegate all this to mere memories?

Before leaving the subject of barns and so on, I must mention the occasion when Father bought the Boyd Farm, so called. This was one of the largest and most productive farms in town and had a considerable and impressive history in its own right. As a boy Father had worked there, one of his jobs being to care for the peacocks they had in the flower gardens about the yard. He had resolved then that some day he would like to own the place himself.

At length, along about 1927, the day came when the place was up at auction and Father decided that here was his opportunity. Accordingly, he climbed into his old Buick and went down to attend the sale. He had had his teeth out a few days before and in his rather shabby shipyard clothes and dusty old car he didn't look particularly like a man in a position to buy that farm. As he put in his first bid the auctioneer regarding him with some disdain said,

"Mister, you realize, I suppose, that you'll have to have the money to pay for this if you're going to bid on this property."

"Young man," said Father, "I'll have you know that I don't set out to buy something without being prepared to pay for it!"

He bought the farm and paid cash for it on the spot.

From the time of my earliest recollection Father had become quite "set in his ways", as we used to say, and consequently the pattern of daily life for the house as well as for himself was rather firmly established. The day began invariably at 6 A.M. when he arose and after dressing, went out to the barn to feed and take care of the horse. He would not put on his regular shoes until after this job was done, wearing instead a special pair of old leather slippers, which smelled strongly of horse, manure and which he frequently left lying on Mother's living room rug. After returning from the barn he would seat himself in his Morris chair and for ten or fifteen minutes would read aloud from the Bible.

By this time Mother would have come downstairs and after taking care of her fires would put some water on to boil and go back to get dressed. Meanwhile, the iceman came, the milkman came, and on Tuesdays and Fridays the fish man. Our fish man was a venerable fellow named Clarence Cook, known to all as "Curly" for his ample curly white mane on top of which he always wore the traditional countryman's black felt cap with the earlaps tied together on top by a black bow. He made his rounds in a closed-in type of wagon that had a sort of shelter with a visor over in front where he sat. He would announce his coming by sounding a loud note on the tin horn he carried by his side. As he drew up in front of our house Mother would holler out the bedroom window to inquire what he had and what the price would be. Then while he was cutting and weighing it, she would slip quickly downstairs and leave a plate and the money on the kitchen shelf. Mr. Cook would bring in the fish, slide it onto the plate and quietly depart. He had a brother, Frank, from whom we always bought our clams.

At about quarter of seven came Sammy Gray to do the chores and take Jimmie the horse, to the shipyard. Sammy was a jovial and lusty man attired in denim jumper and rubber boots whose noisy and cheerful arrival was a welcome event each morning. He took out the ashes, brought up Mother's kitchen coal, and got the fresh bucket of drinking water from the pump down the street in front of my Aunt Julia's house. Along with the chores was usually an item or two of local news or gossip to keep things interesting. Sammy also doubled as a baby sitter for me. I was delighted to have him come since he would often take me downtown with him or would let me get up again if I had gone to bed. Everyone in town knew Sammy. His shouts of greeting could be heard all over the neighborhood and the children and dogs came running. He had no family of his own. Curiously, many who knew him for years never realized his proper name was George P. Gray. He was just "Sammy". Everyone knew who was meant.

In the shipyard Sammy worked with the horse, pulling the timbers from the field into the sawmill. At other times he painted or puttied. Shipyard scrap was sawed up into furnace size chunks and sold for firewood, and another of Sammy's jobs was to take the wagon and deliver the loads. At four o'clock, when work in the yard was over, he would throw on a pile of chunks and, with a shout to us kids, would help us to the top of the load. Then off we'd go with poor old Jimmie struggling to move about as much weight of kids as of wood. If the street where we were going had a hill, Sammy had us get off and walk, but it was worth it, for on the ride home he would give Jimmie a larrup or two with the reins and away we'd go at a gallop.

It was Father's custom to go down to the shipyard at seven to start the gang off. Then, after a little while, he would come home for breakfast, do a little bookkeeping, maybe make a phone call (there was never a telephone at the yard and then go back for the rest of the forenoon. Dinnertime came at twelve o'clock on the dot. After enjoying a leisurely meal it was Father's invariable custom to stretch out on the living room sofa for a half-hour nap. Observation of my 6-foot father in this attitude of repose led me to become a fairly accurate judge of distance, since all I had to do was imagine how many "Pas-lying-down" were contained in a given length.

The workday ended at four o'clock. Father would stop at Percy Burnham's store, pick up his Gloucester Daily Times and then come home to read it. He didn't have to worry about the horse in the evening, because Sammy took care of that when he came in from his last load of wood. Six o'clock was suppertime. Please note that in Essex, the evening meal is, and always was, supper. None of this dinner business at night. Our big meal came at noon. Supper was of a rather light nature and usually included some thing on the order of toast and pear sauce. Again I would like to call attention to the fact that preserved fruits served in a dish constituted sauce; hence, the small dishes they were served in were sauce dishes.

108

After supper Father's first job was to mark the time book for the day, after which he resumed his seat in the Morris chair for an evening of reading He was an avid reader and read almost everything he could find. My parents were not much for going out in the evening, although they did enjoy an occasional bridge game with some of their friends. There was for a while a small movie house in town and perhaps every couple of weeks they would go down to the first show. If it was a Harold Lloyd picture or some thing else fit to see I was allowed to go along.

When I was a child, for some reason Father seemed to take it upon himself to put me to bed. This ritual was always concluded with my recitation of the child's prayer beginning, "Now I lay me down to sleep." Occasionally I would take on a streak of stubbornness and refuse to say my prayers, whereupon Father would snap my ear with his big fingers and growl ever more menacingly, "Say your prayers, boy! (SNAP!) I tell you, say your prayers!!" (SNAP!) Mother, sitting downstairs and listening to the whole procedure, would remark when he finally came down.

"Pa, don't you think that's a funny way to get the boy to say his prayers?"

Saturday night was Father's night to go down to the 20th Century Club. The clubrooms were upstairs over Percy Burnham's store at the foot of our street. Here, as I have said, would gather a group of local men for an evening of cards and comradeship. They had lots of good times up there. Sometimes they made themselves a chowder and enjoyed a good feed. If any chowder was left over, Mr. Oville Chester Story, known to all as "Chink," could usually be counted on to slip in the next day and finish it up. In anticipation of this, Joe Goodhue and a couple of others caught a mouse one night and dropped it into the kettle. Sure enough Chink came in the next day looking for the chowder. Imagine his chagrin at finding that mouse in the bottom of his plate of chowder.

We have spoken in an earlier chapter of Charlie Sam, the town wit. Charlie was an enthusiastic member of the club, but he lived too close for real comfort— his house was next door. When she felt he'd been over there long enough, his wife would lean out an upstairs window and ring an old school bell for him to come home.

In the relatively short span of my lifetime it is interesting to note the changes that have come about in home and community life. One of the things we miss nowadays is the succession of vend ors who used to appear at the house. Some were seasonal, some came once or twice a week; others came every day.

In spring and fall came the "ladder" man with his big load of all kinds of wooden ladders. We used to say that the ladder man would also bring rain.

About the same time the scissors grinder would come through town pushing his grindstone on wheels and calling out his presence. There was also an umbrella man who came around, and let's not forget the man with the hurdy-gurdy.

I have spoken of Mr. Cook the fish man who came on Tuesday and Friday, but we also had Lyman James, the grocer, who came twice a week in his 1914 Model T; there was George Hart in his butcher cart, and Carlie Lampropoulous the banana man who, they said, had forty-'leven kids; then there was T. Morris, the junk man, and Phil Melanson, the ice man, who wore a kind of heavy prickly wool pants, which looked to me about ½ inch thick. We kids, of course, crowded around his wagon to get pieces of ice to suck on. In the summer there was an ice cream man who drove around occasionally and every day, winter and summer, came Deacon Caleb M. Cogswell with the milk. Last, but by no means least, was Will Sundberg who came every Sunday morning in a magnificent Steams-Knight touring car to bring us our Boston Sunday Herald.

Our house always seemed to have a profusion of interesting characters in or about it. First to come on every day, as I have mentioned, was Sammy the chore man. Then there were various men from the yard who came in from time to time on personal errands (usually to borrow money from Father), or maybe it would be an insurance man or a stock and bond salesman. Often we had Mr. Stanton, the paperhanger, at the dinner table, and once in a while there was a dressmaker, Mrs. Clark, who appeared. She occasionally stayed for several days. Sometimes a captain would call at the house to talk about a new vessel. (If he came on Sunday Father would shoo him away.) I'll never forget the night when Capt. Frank N--- called at the house to talk about a new boat. He stayed quite a while and was rather "lit" when he arrived. Before leaving, he went out and spit in the kitchen sink. I thought my mother would go through the ceiling.

A man whom we called Dirty Johnson appeared at the kitchen door one morning with Father who invited him in and asked Mother to get him something to eat. He had come looking for work and had related a long and melancholy hard luck story including one episode in which he "walked to the Philippine Islands," and another in which a freight car bearing all his belongings had gone through an open drawbridge near Portland, Maine. With a wry face Mother prepared something and after gingerly setting it before him retired to the living room, shutting the door behind her. After "Dirty" had left, she picked up his dishes and silverware and put them into boiling water for the rest of the forenoon. When Father came home for dinner he was instructed in no uncertain terms never to bring that man into her house again.

Poor Mother couldn't win, for it wasn't long after that when old Benny Travers, the expressman, came to see Father one evening. He also was feeling good, as they used to say, and before long had overstayed his endurance to the point of wetting his pants while sitting in one of her best over-stuffed chairs. We had to get rid of the chair.

Nothing like this ever bothered Father, who was hardly what you'd call finicky. He had false teeth and after washing his hands in the basin in the sink would take out first his upper plate and then his lower plate and swash them vigorously in the soapy water, shake them off and shove them back in. We were about to have some barley soup one day when Mother spied some weevils in it. With a groan of dismay and revulsion she started for the garbage pail.

"Here, what are you going to do with that?" said Father.

"What am I going to do? Throw it away, of course," was the reply.

"Throw it away, nothing," said Father. "Bring it here and give it to me. We're not going to waste good soup!"

Both Father and Mother had a large number of relatives, many of whom called frequently at our house. It used to be that when relatives called they stayed several days or at least overnight. There was Uncle Jacob, who always told me jokes and funny stories and who never brought so much as a toothbrush when he stayed overnight. Then there was Uncle Bert, Cousin Lucy, Cousin Emma, Aunt Josie, and best of all, Cousin "Willie" Bowlen. He was a great big jovial man who wore a Van Dyke beard, had a large family and drove a Franklin "air-cooled" sedan. Cousin Will had retired from the silver business and seemed to know how to enjoy life. Best of all, he was a fine artist and could usually be counted on to draw me a few sketches of railroad locomotives. He was passionately fond of clam chowder and had a standing order with Mother to serve it whenever he came. In fact, we had a special spoon which he had made and which was inscribed "Clam Chowder Spoon". Cousin Will had driven several times across the country back in the days when it was quite an undertaking and many were the happy evenings we spent listening to tales of his adventures along the way.

So it went. For all of the fact there were only three of us who lived there, there seldom seemed to be a time when at least one other person wasn't in the house for something, either as a visitor or on business of some sort. People of all kinds and from all walks of life found reason to call at our house and it made life there interesting and often exciting. As I look back I can see how they mirrored the way of life in our small town of Essex in years gone by.

Father's real life was his shipyard. He had a large family and loved them all, yet his whole being and existence revolved about the shipyard. He had many business interests, but it was the shipyard that dominated all. My mother, in the later years, would try to coax him away for a little trip or a vacation, but he never would stay. Maybe three or four days he could last and then it was back to the yard. He felt his presence was needed there, and moreover, he felt a very deep sense of obligation to his men and even to the community to keep things going. He took many boats to build knowing full well he might never get paid. If no orders were immediately forthcoming he would build a vessel "on speculation". Sooner or later he always managed to sell it. It was important to him, as he said to keep the gang going. The men realized this and respected him for it and also because of this, most of the better men found fairly steady employment in Arthur's yard.

As might be expected among a gang of men, many of whom had worked together for years, a sort of comradeship or family feeling grew up—perhaps one might almost call it an esprit de corps. This is not meant to imply that all was forever sweetness and light among the men; that there was not an occasional row or disagreement along the way. Hardly—yet generally speaking, the men got on well together and managed to have a good time at their work. I have spoken previously about the fact that most of the shipyard men had a sense of humor and such was certainly the case in Father's yard. He was not a hard man to work for and ran the business with as few words as possible. He didn't interfere with a man who knew his work and was doing it, asking only a good day's work for a day's pay. There was not a time, however, even though he didn't say much, that he was not aware of just what every man was doing. He held the theory, however, that he should only have to tell a man once what he wanted done.

It is a curious side-light to note that while A.D. Story built 425 vessels and knew exactly how every phase of the work should be done, he had absolutely no ability himself as a carpenter. In fact, I cannot recall ever seeing him so much as drive a nail.

With several yards doing business in town at the same time, I have never heard of any bitterness or ill feeling among them. The rivalry was a friendly one. Yards bid on vessels on the basis of the "carpenter's ton", a somewhat arbitrary unit of cubic measure evolved over the years. (It was not an indication of weight.) A yard would build a vessel for so much a carpenter's ton. Actually a genuine spirit of co-operation prevailed among the builders. Tools and equipment were borrowed from one another and sometimes even the men. It was not uncommon for one yard to help another turn up a heavy keel. When Father's big three-master, the *Nat L. Gorton* fell down in launching, Mr. Everett James was glad to send part of his gang over to help with the mess. They came over again to help wedge up the giant steam trawler *Seal* prior to launching, and Father, in turn, sent his men over to help Mr. James when he launched the *Walrus*, a sister ship to the Seal. Both vessels, by the way, were built for the same firm during the first War, and since they were needed in a hurry and one yard alone could not get them out in time, one contract was given to Mr. James and the other to Father. They registered about 480 gross tons apiece and were nearly 170 feet long.

"A.D." built many interesting boats. There were, of course, the hundreds of fishing vessels, and also there were yachts, little freighters, tugs, passenger steamers, government patrol boats, and one was a large steamer designed for salvage work in New York harbor. This last, the *Helen M. Field*, was ready to go in December of 1903 but the river froze and she had to wait until March.

In 1898 he built a patrol steamer, the *Lexington* for the Commonwealth of Massachusetts. This boat of 122 feet in length, 22 foot beam and 9 foot draft was designed for general coast patrol service, particularly against the so-called "porgie pirates." (Porgies are a kind of small herring-like fish.) Bids for the construction of the Lexington were the subject of a lively controversy at the Massachusetts State House after the award had been made to Father. Some of the large yards in and about Boston who were after the job themselves had said he was incapable of maintaining his agreement to deliver the boat in 125 days. Essex yards, they said, did not have the ability or the credit to do a job of this kind. The award was therefore held up in the Governor's Council for several weeks while hearings were held on the subject.

At length the contract was approved and Father undertook the $50,000 job. He not only kept the agreement but also turned out a very efficient boat that exceeded the design requirements in some respects. The keel was laid on May 20, 1898, launching took place on July 28 and by September 6 the Commonwealth had its steamer, a total of 109 calendar days. Bear in mind that several other vessels were under construction in the yard at the same time. It is interesting to note that 26 years later he launched another boat for the Massachusetts police—the *Protector*.

Among the boats he launched in 1900 were two steamers. One was the *Cape Cod*, a large summer excursion boat which ran from Boston to Provincetown, and the other, although starting out as a little coastal freighter, was taken over by the missionary society and, as the *Morning Star*, sailed away to the islands of the South Pacific paid for by the pennies, nickels and dimes of Sunday School pupils all over the country.

Several of Fathers' boats were built to his own account. A 150-ton lighter, the *Margery*, named for his first wife and launched in 1893, was used to transport granite. In 1895 he built a twin-screw steamer called the *John Wise*, named for the illustrious colonial patriot and first minister of Chebacco. This 275 gross ton vessel was used in the marine construction business and also to transport stone. In 1919 he built a 400-ton three-masted schooner called the *Lincoln* that transported lumber and coal between the Maritime Provinces and the United States ports of New York, Boston and Portland. This schooner was rammed and sunk in 1928 at which time Father completed and put into operation a sister ship, the *Adams*.

Among the yachts he built were several that had interesting careers. In 1916 there was the large ketch *Finback*. She was built to the same model as the able schooners *Knickerbocker* and *Catherine*. On launching day a caterer was brought in and a big spread laid amongst the chips and piles of lumber. When she finally slid down the ways she almost didn't make it, her keel digging into the mud so that she nearly stopped. The *Mariner*, built in 1922 for a Mr. Norris of California, was shortly sold to the famous actor, John Barrymore.

A bagpipe band showed up for the launching of the *Argyll* in March 1924. A clipping about the event tells of the raw east wind that whistled under the skirts of these unfortunate gentlemen. The Navigator, built in 1926, found her way to the Philippines, and in 1932, the *Jessie Goldthwait*, which by the way, was the last vessel completed by A.D. Story, was given to Dr. Grenfell's mission in Labrador. The owner's wife had passed away shortly before the yacht was done and he felt he wanted nothing more to do with the boat.

Unquestionably the ships of greatest interest and excitement that Father built were the beautiful schooners that went on to race the Canadian vessels for the coveted International Fishermen's Trophy. The first of these, the *Elsie*, was launched in 1910. Together with the Essex-built schooner *Esperanto* launched by James and Tarr in 1906, they were the only genuine working schooners out of Gloucester to race. The others, while great schooners and vessels that went fishing, were built to be racers. The *Elsie*, although a great little vessel, was pitted against the new and much larger *Bluenose* and didn't stand much of a chance. In one race she carried away her whole foretopmast.

In 1922 Father built the schooner *Henry Ford*. This boat was built to race. She met the Canadian *Bluenose* in the fall of that year for a series of three races off Gloucester and actually beat her. However, a hassle over rules and the size of the *Ford*'s mainsail induced the Committee to award the cup to the Canadians.

Gloucesterites who remembered the details of the event argued for years about the circumstances surrounding this contest. To our family, the *Henry Ford* was remembered as the vessel cast adrift by the towboat as she was being taken to Gloucester. I have never fully understood how it came about, but she was allowed to fetch up on Coffin's Beach and came to rest right between two outcroppings of ledge. Luckily, two of Father's men who were aboard to steer and handle lines were able to get ashore without injury. The ship suffered some damage before a pair of heavy Boston tugs finally pulled her off.

The *Columbia* was another racer launched the following year, 1923. To my mind she was the most graceful and beautiful schooner of them all. Actually, she proved to be the last unpowered salt banker built in Essex. According to the rules, a schooner, though built for racing, had to put in a certain number of months as a working fishermen before she could qualify. The *Columbia*, launched on April 17, was immediately towed to Gloucester where three and a half hours after arriving her spars were stepped and rigging begun. She was a mecca for hundreds of spectators and sightseers as she lay at her wharf outfitting as a dory handliner. On April 26 she sailed on her maiden trip, returning in just two months with

The racing schooner *Henry Ford* came down the ways in 1922. It has been said that she was defeated by the Race Committee rather than the *Bluenose*.

a fare of 324,000 lbs. of salt cod. The maiden stock was $12,693, from which each crewman shared $261.00. In September she brought in her second trip—225,000lbs. of salt cod. After a few last minute preparations and a warm-up race with some sister schooners off Gloucester, she sailed for Halifax where she was to meet the *Bluenose* on October 29. The first race, won by *Bluenose*, was protested since the *Bluenose* had seriously fouled *Columbia*. The second race was again won by *Bluenose* but her captain sailed away in a huff over the protesting of the first race by *Columbia*. No third race was sailed. The committee therefore awarded the trophy to *Columbia*, but her skipper, Captain Ben Pine, declined to accept it under those circumstances. The *Columbia* raced once more in October 1926 when she defeated the *Henry Ford* in two hometown races off Gloucester. The end came for *Columbia* in the great gale of August 24, 1927 when she went down with all hands off Sable Island, the graveyard of countless ships.

No account of Father's vessels would be complete without speaking briefly of the well known *Gertrude L. Thebaud,* This last of the great schooners, racing or otherwise, was launched on Saint Patrick's day in 1930. The publicity generated by her building brought a great crowd to witness the event and even occasioned the closing of the public schools in order that the youngsters might enjoy the fun and excitement. The vessel was paid for by Mr. Louis Thebaud, a wealthy sportsman and summer resident of Gloucester. He caused beautifully embossed, emerald and gold invitations to be sent to his friends announcing the great event. The skipper of the *Thebaud* was to be the celebrated Captain Ben Pine.

The launching, fortunately, was eminently successful and the Boston papers were filled with its account. Mr. Thebaud felt it was important that Gloucester should bring home the cup by fairly and squarely defeating the *Bluenose*.

The two vessels met on three occasions. The first, in October 1930, saw the *Thebaud* winner in three straight races. Unfortunately, the cup was not at stake on this occasion. The second series took place the following year off Halifax, and this time for the cup. Now it was *Bluenose*'s turn and she took it with three straight. The last of all fishermen's races took place in October 1938 off Gloucester. Five races were run with *Bluenose* winning three of the five. The *Thebaud* had an interesting career quite aside from her racing. She carried a large delegation of prominent Gloucester skippers to Washington in April 1933 to plead the cause of the Gloucester fishing industry, then at a very low ebb. She was met at the dock by F. D. R. himself, accompanied by none other than Prime Minister Ramsay MacDonald of Great Britain. In July of the same year she sailed to Chicago to become the official exhibit of the Commonwealth of Massachusetts at the

The Schooner *Columbia* leaves Essex in tow for Gloucester where she was fitted out.

Chicago World's Fair. While at the fair she averaged 2,500 visitors a day. Also at the fair was her old rival *Bluenose*.

In the summer of 1937 the noted Arctic explorer, Commander Donald MacMillan, chartered the *Thebaud* for a scientific cruise into the waters of Frobisher Bay. A crew of 37 was aboard, including several professors and students. After many adventures, including one that nearly lost the vessel, she returned home, having traveled over 8,000 miles.

During the Second World War, the *Thebaud* was taken by the U. S. Coast Guard as a patrol boat and was so used until 1944 when she was returned to her owners and sold as a freighter for use in the Caribbean. In 1948 she went to her last resting place against a stone breakwater in Venezuela. So ended a great era for Essex as well as for Gloucester.

It is not my intention to create the impression that A.D. Story was the only Essex man to build racing schooners. I have spoken of the valiant *Esperanto* built by James and Tarr. She was doubtless the gamest of the lot, since with little more than a fresh coat of paint she left for Halifax in October of 1920 and soundly defeated the Canadian champion *Delawana*. A thrilling maneuver in the second race saw the *Esperanto* almost run onto the beach by the Canadians, but the intrepid *Marty Welch*, her skipper, held his course and it was the Canadian who finally gave way. The attempted trick actually cost the race for the *Delawana*.

Other racers built in the James yard were *Mayflower* in 1921, and Puritan in 1922. Informed opinion maintains that *Mayflower* was the fastest racing schooner ever built, though there are some who will vigorously dispute this. In order to meet the qualifying deadline, the *Mayflower*, a big schooner of 165 gross tons and some 140 feet on deck, was completed in 59 working days from keel to launching, which affair was the biggest public event ever held in town. In spite of the efforts and expense of the Boston syndicate that built her, she was disqualified and barred from racing by the international committee. They claimed she was a yacht. A few informal brushes with qualified contenders, American and Canadian, demonstrated the *Mayflower* to be much the faster.

Puritan was another big schooner (149 gross tons) and extremely fast, but she never had a chance. On her third trip she piled onto Sable Island, a total loss. At the time, the vessel was only three months old.

Any study of the facts concerning the conduct of the International fishermen's races will reveal an astonishing lack of sportsmanship and often just plain bad manners on the part of the Canadian contenders. The most elemental rules of sailboat racing, which any yachtsman accepts as a matter of course, were openly flouted, and what seemed worse were flouted with the apparent blessing of the race committee. The record would indicate, as an extreme example, that in the races of the *Henry Ford* and *Bluenose* in 1922 that it was the committee that defeated the *Ford*. In fairness, however, it must be stated that this particular committee was composed of a majority of American members. In short, what could have been a series of sporting spectacles of the grandest dimensions and an exciting example of friendly national rivalry for all the world to see, was reduced in too many cases by pettiness, mean selfish interest and gamblers, to a level of childish squabbles.

For all his feverish boat building activity and divergent business interests, Father's finances weren't much more than a hand-to-mouth affair in the early years. I have heard him tell how as a young man was just starting out and with a new family to support he sat one evening with his wife while they idly speculated on how they might best use their last ten dollar bill. As they talked quietly in the kitchen of their upstairs tenement, footsteps were heard coming up the stairs. Answering the knock, they found old Dr. Lovering outside. "I was wondering," he said, "if you could see your way clear to pay me for that last baby I delivered." There went the $10.00.

Mr. E. H. Oxner, who worked for a time as Father's foreman, has told of coming back into the yard after the men had gone home and finding him alone and hunched over with head in hands sitting on an empty keg underneath a vessel. "What am I going to do?" he said. "I've got payrolls to meet and notes coming due and nothing to pay them with!" From the record it would appear that somehow the difficulties were met.

Not all his troubles were financial, as we have seen. The biggest boat Father ever built was a large three-masted ship of 610 gross tons, the *Warwick*. It was when her keel had been set up and some of the frames erected that it was discovered she was six feet too short. Some of the frames had to come down and the keel cut and pieced out. Other frames had to be made which would fair in with existing ones. Somehow they managed and the finished ship showed no sign of what had happened. As John Prince used to say, "There never was a 'bull' made so bad you couldn't get out of it somehow!"

Everyday events in the yard reflected all sorts of triumphs and contortions of the human spirit. There used to be a little man in our yard named Willie Scroons. Willy had white whiskers and always wore one of the heavy black felt caps with the earflaps. He had no family hereabouts and lived alone, so that when he died there was nobody to pay any respects to the deceased. Father felt the poor man should be accorded recognition of some sort, so on the day of the funeral, he knocked off the whole gang and all the shipyard men attended the funeral in a body. Willy, by the way, was buried with his big black cap on.

It was common for Essex boys to head for the shipyards when it became time to look for a job or to fill in for a summer. Two such young men who worked for Father were Harold Burnham and Arthur Doyle. As is often the case, the young fellows were keen in their observation of the way things should be done and especially how much they could get away with. Father called to Harold one day and Arthur, hearing him too, said, "Don't go 'till he hollers three times."

"Why not?"

"Because if he hollers three times, he really means it."

Father would send the boys over to the blacksmith shop with broken augers. Usually they could contrive to stop off somewhere and get some cookies or a light lunch. Imagine their surprise when Father handed them some cookies one morning along with the augers and said, "There boys. You won't need to stop for a lunch this morning."

Father's remarks could be directed with complete impartiality. My uncle Eddie (Edwin J. Story), of whom I have spoken, worked at various times in the yard. I remember him as a molder who lined out the cuts in the timber up on the hillside at the rear of the yard where the oak was spread out. He worked alone for the most part and could wander at will among the piles of timber. It may be that he wasn't getting things lined out fast enough for one day Father approached in some agitation and called out.

"Eddie, ye have compassed this mountain long enough"

Fishermen, in fact sea-faring men of all kinds, have always laid considerable store by superstition, taking great care in the course of their livelihood not to offend the gods or whoever it is that is concerned with those things. The building of vessels and the course of the work in our shipyard was not without the influence of superstition. Father came to work one winter morning decked out in a fine pair of bright red mittens his wife had knit for him. A captain, who happened to be in the yard at the time was much upset and asked that he take them off at once since, as he said, they presaged ill fortune for the vessels. Much impressed, Father did as he was told and from that day forward it was forbidden to wear red mittens in our yard.

Another of the great shipyard superstitions was that a hatch cover, once made, should never be turned bottom up. Care should always be taken in moving or setting them aside that they remain right side up.

Lastly, it was important that a new keel must not be turned up and set in place on Friday. Keels are made from many pieces and considerable work is involved. They are usually made upside down and when finished are rolled or turned up. Although other operations could take place at any time, the new keel was not to be rolled up on Friday. By the same token, it was never planned to launch the new boat on Friday and when she sailed on her maiden trip it could be on any day but Friday. Much as we hear of "the exceptions that prove the rule", were the few skippers who took the opposite stand and insisted that for them the new keel must be turned on Friday and the boat launched on Friday.

So it went. The every day life in the shipyards carried on day by day, year by year for generations. The sounds of the yards, the coming and going of the men, the launchings and all the rest that went with it were almost taken for granted. That was Essex. Then, almost as if a switch had been thrown, it was all over. The year was 1932, one of trial and hardship in many parts of the world. We had been building vessels fairly steadily right along through the first years of the depression, when suddenly it appeared that no more orders were forthcoming either for our yard or for the James yard, which were the only two still operating.

On Saturday, February 27, 1932, Father launched a small dragger, *the Carlo and Vince*. The following day he was taken sick. It tuned out to be a recurrence of his old heart trouble. He took to his bed and never went to his shipyard again. Death came on March 5. My half-brother Jacob who had been working with Father in the yard for ten years or more took over and completed the remaining vessels. One, the *Grace F.*, was already finished and was launched on March 12, and the other, the yacht *Jessie Goldthwait*", was nearly done and was launched on April 20. Father had laid a new keel the week before he was taken sick and this vessel was built by brother Jacob who launched her in July.

It was a curious coincidence that on the day of Father's death Mr. Everett James completed and launched his last vessel, the *Sebastiana C.* Furthermore, although brother Jacob had taken over our yard, not a single vessel was built in Essex the following year. One little tug was built in 1934 and in 1935, again nothing. The years from 1935 to 1949 saw a brief resurgence of building, with even three yards operating in the winter of 1946-1947. But then with the launching of the little schooner *Eugenia J.* by Jonathan Story in June 1949, the end came for good.

I do not hesitate to say that the impact of A.D. Story's passing on the town of Essex was considerable. The following excerpt from the *Gloucester Daily Times* of Tuesday, March 8, 1932, three days after his death, is quoted in part:"The 113th Annual Town Meeting of Essex was called to order last evening at 7:30 with Moderator Honorable W. W. Lufkin in the chair and Grover N. Dodge acting clerk."

A description of introductory remarks and the invocation followed, after which and quoting again: "Lester Tompkins, Chairman of the Board of Selectmen, then offered a motion: 'Out of respect to the late Honorable Arthur Dana Story, one who has been a most respected citizen and a constant contributor to the best interests and welfare of this town, I move that his name be honored by ceasing deliberation at this time, and that this meeting stand adjourned until Friday evening, March 11, at 7:30 o'clock, and I further move that a committee of five be appointed by the moderator to draw up resolutions on the death of Mr. Story and that these be spread on the town records and a copy be sent to the family of the deceased.' This was unanimously voted. The meeting was then adjourned until Friday evening. This was the first time in the history of the town, as far as can be recalled, that a town meeting had been adjourned on account of the death of a private citizen."

The resolutions drawn up as a result of this motion are impressive in their content. I quote them here:

"Arthur Dana Story—Born October 11, 1854, died March 5, 1932, native, lifelong resident and lover of the town of Essex and its people; for nearly 60 years creator of the most advanced types and construction of the finest fishing vessels to sail the seven seas; devout in his support of the religious life of the community; a leader in the civic affairs of the town and enjoying the confidence and respect of the leaders of his party in the state and in the nation; of striking integrity in both his personal and business dealings; a descendant of the Pilgrims who landed at Plymouth Rock in 1620; a splendid example of the courage and persistence of the men and women of that historic pilgrimage; quiet but forceful; stern and austere in appearance but warmhearted and affectionate in action. Arthur Dana Story exemplified to the last degree, not only the spirit and life of his early ancestors, but that rapidly disappearing type in the community, 'The New England Gentleman of the Old School!'"